TURKISH FLAVOURS

SEVTAP YÜCE

TURKISH FLAVOURS

RECIPES FROM A SEASIDE CAFÉ

hardie grant books
MELBOURNE · LONDON

SBS

CONTENTS

FROM ANKARA TO ANGOURIE

GROWING UP IN TURKEY

My father moved to Ankara to work when he was sixteen, and I was born there. As a little girl, I used to follow my mother, *anne*, around the kitchen watching everything she did, and first started cooking when I was about six years old. When she made flatbread, I would steal pieces of the dough and try to make a small loaf out of them. When she made biscuits (cookies), I would try to make a few on each tray. My father, *baba*, would come home from work and say, 'Are you still making biscuits?', which we made all the time.

There were four children in my family, and we were very poor. Despite this we always ate very well. Two hundred and fifty grams (nine ounces) of minced (ground) meat would last our family for four days. I remember being sent to the butcher to buy minced meat for the family when I was seven years old. I noticed the butcher ran the meat through the mincer twice, and when I asked why, he explained that it was to hide the fat. To this day, I closely watch the butcher to make sure he's not running the meat through twice.

Me, aged seven (top right), with my sister Güfer (aged twelve), brother Murat (aged five) and brother Ferhat (aged three)

Most people in Turkey were poor when I was a child; we didn't know anything different. My family are *Alevi* Muslim. We don't fast during Ramadan, we fast at a different time, *Muharrem Ayi*. During this time we would fast for two weeks. At the end of the fasting, families would slaughter a sheep or a rooster, depending on how wealthy they were, and then take the best portions to share with their poorest neighbours.

At this time everyone would hold a feast for their family. If we had a sheep, Anne would smoke the legs and the head of the sheep to remove the hair, then clean and boil them, and make a soup with fresh garlic. Every part of the animal would be eaten. We would fry the sheep's testicles, the kidneys and liver. The brains would be made into a salad, drizzled with lemon juice and olive oil.

When I was a small child my father sold fruit and vegetables, similar to a wholesaler. Later he opened a café, or *kahvane*. Only men were allowed in the *kahvane*, where they would play cards or backgammon and drink tea all day. There was no food in the *kahvane*, just coffee, tea and apple tea (*tarçin*). I would dress up as a boy and serve cups of tea. I was paid five cents a day for this work, but my brother and his friends worked there too, and they were paid fifteen cents a day.

We didn't have access to clean running water from the tap – we had plumbing, but the water would freeze solid in winter. An old man would deliver our water on a donkey every couple of days. He seemed very old to me, and I felt sorry for him riding along in the cold on his donkey. One day I saw him at my father's *kahvane*, so I took the donkey home to deliver our water myself and save the old man a trip. On my way I was stopped by a neighbour, who asked if this was the new owner of the *kahvane*. I said, 'No uncle, he's our new neighbour!'

Anne and Baba in the 1970s

The women in Turkey spent hours cooking, because everything was made from scratch – even the filo pastry. My grandparents grew wheat, and my uncle grew vine leaves, and when they harvested we were given bags of this produce to last us through the winter.

I remember Anne making baklava. First she would soak the wheat for a couple of days, and the sediment would collect underneath. She would keep the sediment, which was fine like cornflour (cornstarch), then dry it, and sprinkle it over each sheet of the pastry. The best baklava is still made this way; it's a hundred times better than mine.

We made flatbread in summer to be used during the winter. The breads were stored in stacks to dry out, and then when winter came we would sprinkle them with water and heat them through to eat.

When I was about seven or eight years old, I started cutting out recipes from the newspaper and pasting them into a book. I filled the book with recipes and carried it with me for many years, even to Australia. But when my house in Leichhardt burned down, the book burned with it. I was so sad.

My grandparents all lived about four hours away in a little village near Çhorum called Karkin Koyü.

I called my mother's stepfather Buýuk baba. He sold animals for a living. One day when he came home with buffaloes, I was so scared that I hid. My grandmother, Anneanne, would milk the buffaloes he brought home and make yoghurt from the milk. She would boil the milk, then cool it. When she tested the milk with her little finger and it held for five seconds without burning her finger, it was ready. Next she would take a bit of the old yoghurt and mix it with the hot milk, then pour it back into the pot, stir it and put a lid on it. She would cover the pot with all the blankets and jumpers we had, for about eight hours, then uncover it and cut out the yoghurt with a knife.

Babaanne and Dede, my paternal grandparents, around 1980

Babaanne and Dede were my father's parents. Babaanne would make yoghurt from cow's milk or sheep's milk, then put it into a *yayik*, a wooden cask with a lid and a little hole. The cask would hang from the ceiling like a swing. Babaanne would sit on one end and I would sit on the other, and we would rock it backwards and forwards until the butter formed on top. She would scoop out the butter, then wash it. We would have the butter on our bread, and drink the juice from the yoghurt.

I remember one day when I was a child and we were having a picnic, Dede took a watermelon, cut out the pulp and made shepherd's salad. It's made with tomatoes, cucumbers, green capsicums (peppers) and olive oil. He tossed all the salad together and then piled it back into the watermelon shell. That was the only time I ever saw my grandfather cook.

Dede had a *seten*, a big rock and wheel, used for husking the grain from wheat after harvesting. He would roll and smoke his cigarettes, then draw the horse through the fields. All the villagers would bring their grain to him, and he would grind it with the *seten*, to make cracked wheat.

There's a black and white photo of Babaanne and Dede hanging on the wall at Beachwood. It was taken around 1980, and it tells a lot about life and people in Turkey even then. Babaanne is holding one of her pots of yoghurt, and Dede is smoking one of his roll-up cigarettes. They are dressed in coats, standing near a whitewashed house with a wooden doorframe. Dede is in front, scowling at the camera, with a lined face and a bushy moustache. Babaanne has a headscarf and is wearing shoes and stockings, with a beautiful wide smile on her face.

THE TURKISH MARKETPLACE

Good Turkish cooking is all about the ingredients. When I was a girl, there was a little growers' marketplace in our neighbourhood every Monday or Wednesday. My sister and I would walk from one end of the market to the other, chatting with the stall holders and buying our food for the next few days. One stall holder sold eggplants (aubergines), one sold potatoes, one had a stall with all the greens and tomatoes, another a stall with peaches, and so on. At the end of the line of fresh produce stalls were the spice stalls, then sardines and watermelons.

Every neighbourhood in Ankara had a market. One day it would be at Maltepe, then the next day it would be in Etlik, and then the next in Ingirli. In Turkey, each area is famous for certain produce. Çorum is famous for chickpeas, Malatya for apricots, Kayseri for pastrami, Bursa for chestnuts, Rize for tea, and Izmir for grapes. Growers travelled around to each of the areas selling their produce, so you could get a little of everything in each neighbourhood.

I have a photo of a man selling his chillies on the road outside the markets, because he couldn't afford a stall. He is in his seventies, and his chillies are lined up on the ground on a cloth. This is the way to buy chillies – fresh from the market, from someone who has lovingly grown them. Turkish chillies, *biber*, grow about twenty centimetres (eight inches) long. There are different varieties, from sweet to mildly hot, in varying degrees of heat. Hot chillies are *açi* and sweet chillies are *tatli*. You can cook them on the barbecue, pan-fry them in oil, or eat them raw. They are a part of the daily diet in Turkey, and are eaten for breakfast, lunch and dinner. I come home from work some days and eat fresh chillies from my garden with tomatoes, parsley and feta. In Turkey there are maybe ten different kinds of feta, used for different dishes. I always eat Bulgarian feta in Australia, because it's the best.

SETTLING IN AUSTRALIA

When I finished high school in Turkey, I worked in accounting because Baba thought I should study. Coming from a poorer family, he wanted me to make something out of my life. Accounting was good, but I didn't have the ingredients I loved in front of me – the cucumber and the tomato, the onion and garlic weren't there.

Baba passed away when I was sixteen. That was just before I was found by the man who brought me to Australia through an arranged marriage. I came to Coburg in Melbourne with him in 1985, when I was just seventeen.

I returned to Turkey in 1986 and then came back to settle in Sydney in November 1986. I worked in Marrickville and Newtown, and worked for Ellea Burneau, who ran a patisserie called Little Devil Temptations. She also taught me how to speak English.

I worked as a waitress in a café in Darlinghurst called Dov from 1990 to 1993. A friend suggested to me that I become a chef. I started studying commercial cookery, and within six months I was running the café. I never finished the commercial cookery course.

In 1994 I was working in Bill Granger's café in Sydney. When we were walking along William Street one day, I told him I had a plan to move to Angourie for a sea change and open a restaurant. He asked me about Angourie, and I said, 'It's beachy and there's lots of wood', and he said, 'What about "Beachwood"?' So that's how my restaurant got its name.

BEACHWOOD

I opened Beachwood at Angourie in 1994, in the Northern Rivers region of New South Wales. Angourie is on the surfing pilgrimage route, a favourite with surfers daring enough to throw themselves

into its huge and unpredictable wave sets, and with tourists who come for the beaches, the national park and the glorious views. I bought my little house at Angourie in 1997, and love to sit watching the kangaroos at dusk.

I had Beachwood in Angourie until 1998, when I moved it to Yamba, initially on the top of the hill, up the road from where it is now. It seated around one hundred people, much larger than today's café.

Beachwood won the best new restaurant award in 1998. Sometimes I am asked why I haven't moved the business to Sydney or Melbourne, but this is home for me. If I lived in Sydney I could never peel enough broad (fava) beans to feed all those people. I live here for the lifestyle and the people, and being part of the community.

I sold Beachwood on the top of the hill in 2002, and went to live in Holland for a few years, but always knew I would return. This place is home to me now.

I opened Beachwood again in High Street, Yamba, in November 2006, and have been there ever since. The High Street café has a tiny kitchen, just four metres by four metres (thirteen feet by thirteen feet), and ten tables comfortably seating about thirty people. It's a vibrant little café, and I love getting to know each of the people who come here, whether they're tourists or locals.

Every day at Beachwood we get fresh produce from local growers. Doug the fisherman rings me at six o'clock every morning and tells me how last night's catch went. Maybe he's got a haul of crabs or prawns (shrimps), and then my challenge is to figure out how to prepare them for lunch.

Yamba is situated at the mouth of the Clarence River, where the river meets the Pacific Ocean. We are spoilt with delicious seafood fresh from its natural habitat, caught by local fishermen.

Kim comes into the café every Friday with no shoes on, and brings me fresh eggs from his chickens, along with lemons, chillies, eggplants (aubergines), parsley and broad (fava) beans. Bob brings fresh sardines from Iluka, and Ben brings chickpeas. There are others who grow tomatoes and cauliflower, and produce their own honey. This means that we can prepare so much of our menu right here at the restaurant, from my kofte to baklava, cakes and even the honeycomb in Baba's honeycomb butter recipe.

The main reason I love to live and work here is the wonderful connection with the people, local farmers and local produce. The food is connected to a face and a story. My customers can see for themselves how fresh and beautiful the local produce is, and then they understand why it tastes so good.

THE KITCHEN GARDEN

When I was young, Baba would dig the garden and Anne would plant it out. I remember coming home from school, starving, when I was seven or eight years old. I would grab bread out of the cupboard and run out to the garden. There would be *tere* (similar to watercress), spring onions (scallions), flat-leaf parsley, mint, dill and green chillies. I would put these in my bread and this would be my snack after school. In our garden there were also tomatoes, cucumbers, cauliflowers, grapes, sour cherries, apricots and plums.

For me, growing my own food is the most rewarding, most important thing – eating out of the earth as you might say. When I first moved to Angourie and couldn't buy what I wanted, I gave a man seeds from Jerusalem artichokes, coriander (cilantro), chilli and rocket (arugula). I said to him, 'If you can grow this for me, I will buy it from you.' One day he rang me, excited because he had a box of rocket.

Beachwood is now well known for its little garden situated right next to the tables. I grow herbs, such as parsley, basil, oregano, thyme, mint, chervil, chives and dill, as well as chillies, eggplants (aubergines), tomatoes, Jerusalem artichokes, asparagus, fennel, capsicums (peppers), ginger, nasturtiums and strawberries. People love to help themselves to the herbs while they're sitting in the sun.

At home in Angourie I have the same plants in my garden. I think you should be able to go out to your garden and pick what you want to eat, put it in bread and eat it. That's what makes me happy.

TURKISH HOSPITALITY

In Holland, if you arrived uninvited at someone's house at dinnertime, it would be acceptable for them to tell you to come back after dinner. But in Turkey, you would be brought inside, and immediately a plate and a glass of *raki* (an alcoholic drink made from aniseed) or tea would be placed in front of you. If you say, 'I'm not hungry', Turkish people will blackmail you into eating, saying, 'If you don't eat, I can't eat and I will never speak to you again', or, 'You have to eat for the love of Allah.' What can you say to that?

This is Turkish hospitality – we love to host families, friends and strangers. Beachwood is my home, and it is the greatest source of joy for me to cook and look after people. I love to share this joy and love of food and hospitality with everyone who comes here.

When I am looking for people to work in my kitchen, I look for people who love food, who truly have a passion for cooking and making food for people to eat. I'm not against commercial training; I have trained several people who are fully qualified chefs now. But even with the best training, I still need to show them how to cook my food, and it's easier to show someone who's excited by food, someone who gets excited by local produce. When a local grower brings me a basket of fresh lemons or peaches, I want people around me who get caught up in the excitement and say, 'Let's make that cake you told me about', or who know that it's one of our customers' birthdays and want to make them something special that they love to eat.

The recipes I have chosen to share in this book are simple and easy to make. That's the joy of Turkish food – it uses fresh produce from your kitchen garden and basic ingredients from your refrigerator and pantry. It takes minimal time to prepare and brings together traditional blends of delicious flavours.

BREAKFAST

IN TURKEY, WHOEVER RISES FIRST MAKES THE TEA. THE
FAMILY COME TOGETHER FOR BREAKFAST, WHICH CAN
LAST FOR HOURS. EVERYONE TAKES A LITTLE OF THIS AND
A LITTLE OF THAT — EGGS, JAMS AND JELLIES, HONEY, FETA,
ONION, OLIVES, TOMATO AND CUCUMBER — AS WELL
AS FRESHLY BAKED CRUSTY WHITE BREAD AND,
OF COURSE, THE TEA.

FLATBREADS WITH TAHINI AND HONEY

MAKES TWELVE

INGREDIENTS

Dough
1 tablespoon active dry yeast
1 tablespoon sugar
2 cups plain (all-purpose) flour
pinch of sea salt

250 ml (8½ fl oz) tahini
3 tablespoons honey
olive oil or butter for brushing

METHOD

To make the dough, mix the yeast and sugar with 80 ml (3 fl oz) warm water and set aside until the yeast starts foaming, about 5 minutes. Combine the flour and salt in a large bowl. Gradually stir in the yeast mixture and about 250 ml (8½ fl oz) warm water to form a soft dough. Knead the dough on a floured board for 10 minutes. The dough should feel like your earlobe. Leave the dough in a warm place for 45 minutes, or until it has doubled in size.

Preheat the oven to 160°C (320°F/Gas 2–3). Divide the dough into 12 balls and set aside for 15 minutes.

Press each dough ball into a 12 cm (4¾ in) circle. Spread the tahini and honey over each circle, then roll up to form a cylinder. Gently stretch each cylinder as you wind it around itself to resemble a snail, then flatten it with a rolling pin until about 1 cm (½ in) thick.

Brush each flatbread with olive oil or butter. Cook in a heavy-based frying pan over medium heat for 3–4 minutes, or until brown. Turn and brown the other side.

Transfer the flatbreads to a baking tray and bake for 10 minutes. Serve hot or at room temperature.

PAN-FRIED FETA BREAD

SERVES TWO

INGREDIENTS

2 eggs

250 ml (8½ fl oz) milk

pinch of sea salt

100 g (3½ oz) Bulgarian feta, crumbled

1 large handful flat-leaf parsley, chopped

50 g (2 oz) butter

4 slices thick white bread, such as Turkish bread or baguette

METHOD

Whisk the eggs, milk and salt in a shallow bowl until combined. Combine the feta and parsley in a separate shallow bowl.

Melt the butter in a frying pan over medium heat. Dip the bread into the egg mixture and then into the feta mixture. Fry the bread until golden, about 5 minutes on each side. Serve hot.

CARAMELISED ONION WITH EGGS

SERVES TWO

INGREDIENTS

2 large red (Spanish) onions
80 g (3 oz) unsalted butter
sea salt
freshly cracked black pepper
4 eggs
crusty bread to serve

METHOD

Cut the onions in half and then into slices. Melt the butter in a large frying pan and cook the onion over low heat, stirring occasionally, for 10–15 minutes, until brown and soft. Take care not to burn the onion. Season with sea salt and freshly cracked black pepper and mix thoroughly.

Make four indentations in the onion with the back of a spoon, and crack an egg into each one. Cover and cook over low heat until the egg whites are cooked through but the yolks are still soft.

Serve the caramelised onion and eggs immediately, with crusty bread and black tea.

VARIATION

Try cooking one or two chopped long green chillies with the eggs or sprinkling them over the top of the finished dish.

SCRAMBLED EGGS WITH FETA AND PARSLEY

SERVES TWO

INGREDIENTS

4 eggs
100 ml (3½ fl oz) single (light)
   cream (35% fat)
pinch of sea salt
3 tablespoons chopped flat-leaf
   parsley
20 g (¾ oz) butter
50 g (2 oz) Bulgarian feta
Turkish bread to serve
sucuk (Turkish sausage) to serve
   (see page 187)

METHOD

Gently whisk the eggs with the cream, salt and parsley.

Melt the butter in a non-stick frying pan over low heat. Pour in the egg mixture and gently fold until just set, about 5 minutes.

Crumble the feta over the eggs and serve immediately, with toasted Turkish bread and pan-fried sucuk.

GARLIC MUSHROOMS

SERVES TWO

INGREDIENTS

50 g (2 oz) butter

250 g (9 oz) button mushrooms, sliced

10 g ($\frac{1}{2}$ oz) dried porcini mushrooms, broken into small pieces

3 garlic cloves, chopped

1 large handful flat-leaf parsley, chopped

sea salt

freshly cracked black pepper

125 ml (4 fl oz) single (light) cream (35% fat)

1 avocado, sliced

Turkish bread to serve

METHOD

Melt the butter in a frying pan over high heat. Add the button mushrooms and porcini mushrooms and cook, stirring constantly, for 10–15 minutes, or until well browned.

Add the garlic and parsley and season with sea salt and freshly cracked black pepper. Cook until the mushrooms are soft, then pour in the cream and stir over low heat for 5 minutes, or until thickened.

Serve the mushrooms hot, with the avocado and toasted Turkish bread.

MENEMEN EGGS

INGREDIENTS

125 ml (4 fl oz) extra-virgin
    olive oil
1 onion, finely diced
1 kg (2 lb 3 oz) tomatoes, peeled
    and diced (see page 185)
1 green capsicum (pepper),
    cut into 1 cm ($^1/_2$ in) cubes
1 green chilli, finely chopped
pinch of sugar
sea salt
freshly cracked black pepper
4 eggs

METHOD

Heat the olive oil in a large saucepan. Fry the onion over medium heat for 10–15 minutes, or until soft but not browned. Add the tomato, capsicum and chilli and cook over low heat for 45 minutes, or until the tomatoes are soft. Add the sugar and season to taste with sea salt and black pepper.

Spoon half the tomato mixture into a large frying pan, then gently crack the eggs into the pan. Cover and cook over low heat until the egg whites are cooked through but the yolks are still soft, about 5 minutes. Serve immediately.

NOTE

Refrigerate the remaining tomato sauce for a few days. Gently reheat the sauce in the frying pan before adding the eggs.

EGGS IN GARLIC YOGHURT

SERVES TWO

INGREDIENTS

50 g (2 oz) butter

4 eggs

250 g (9 oz) garlic yoghurt
   (see page 185)

flatbread to serve

METHOD

Melt the butter in a non-stick frying pan over medium heat. Crack the eggs into the pan, then move them around the pan with a fork until they are just set.

Fold the cooked eggs through the garlic yoghurt. Serve immediately, with flatbread.

FRIED POTATO, TOMATO AND CHILLI

SERVES TWO

INGREDIENTS

sunflower oil for shallow-frying

2 potatoes, cut into 1 cm (½ in) thick strips

6–8 long green chillies

3 tomatoes, peeled and diced (see page 185)

pinch of sea salt

crusty bread to serve

METHOD

Heat the sunflower oil in a frying pan. Fry the potato strips over high heat for 5–6 minutes, or until golden. Drain the potato on paper towel, then transfer to a serving bowl.

Fry the chillies in the same frying pan until browned, about 5 minutes. Add the chillies to the potato.

Drain off all but about 2 tablespoons of the oil from the pan. Add the diced tomato and salt and cook over medium heat until soft, about 5 minutes. Pour the tomato over the potato and chillies, and season with sea salt.

Serve hot with crusty bread and sweet black tea.

NOTE

This is also delicious cold, with garlic yoghurt (see page 185).

BABA'S HONEYCOMB BUTTER

SERVES FOUR

INGREDIENTS

100 g (3$^{1}/_{2}$ oz) hazelnuts
250 g (9 oz) good-quality honey,
  with honeycomb
100 g (3$^{1}/_{2}$ oz) unsalted butter,
  at room temperature

METHOD

Preheat the oven to 160°C (320°F/Gas 2–3). Roast the hazelnuts on a baking tray for 10 minutes, or until fragrant. Rub the hazelnuts in a clean tea towel to remove the skins.

Put the honey and honeycomb, hazelnuts and butter in a bowl and stir until well combined. Spoon the honeycomb butter into sterilised jars (see page 185) and refrigerate for up to 2 weeks.

NOTE

Serve the honeycomb butter with yoghurt, on toast, on its own with coffee, or on pancakes.

I remember waking up to the smell of honeycomb, roasted hazelnuts and butter as Baba lovingly mixed them together. He would give me a spoonful and I'd drift back to sleep, still tasting his honeycomb butter.

POACHED FRUIT WITH YOGHURT

SERVES FOUR

INGREDIENTS

500 g (1 lb 2 oz) rhubarb
500 g (1 lb 2 oz) strawberries
500 g (1 lb 2 oz) pears
1 cup sugar
250 g (9 oz) Greek-style plain
    yoghurt
125 g (4 oz) roasted pistachios,
    crushed

METHOD

Cut the rhubarb into 3 cm (1 in) lengths and trim the stalks from the strawberries. Peel, quarter and core the pears.

Put the rhubarb and strawberries in a frying pan and sprinkle with half the sugar. Cover and cook over high heat until the rhubarb is soft, about 5 minutes.

Meanwhile, put the pears in a non-stick frying pan and sprinkle with the remaining sugar. Cover and cook over high heat until the pears are just tender, about 5 minutes.

Divide the pears among four bowls, then spread the rhubarb and strawberries over the top. Spoon 3 tablespoons of yoghurt into each bowl and sprinkle with the pistachios.

NOTE

Rhubarb reacts with aluminium, so use a stainless steel or non-stick frying pan.

BEACHWOOD WINTER PORRIDGE

SERVES FOUR

INGREDIENTS

200 g (7 oz) rolled oats
500 ml (17 fl oz) milk
2 bananas, sliced
ground cinnamon to serve
honey to serve

METHOD

Soak the rolled oats in 500 ml (17 fl oz) water overnight.

Transfer the oats to a saucepan and pour in the milk. Bring to the boil, then reduce the heat to low. Cook, stirring regularly, for 20 minutes, or until the porridge is thick and creamy.

Divide the porridge among four bowls. Top with the sliced banana and sprinkle with the cinnamon. Drizzle with honey and serve immediately.

VARIATION

For a healthy boost, finely grind 1 tablespoon each of pumpkin seeds, sunflower seeds, linseeds and chia seeds and sprinkle over the porridge.

ROSE PETAL JAM

INGREDIENTS

120 g (4 oz) pesticide-free red
  or pink rose petals
4 cups sugar
2 tablespoons lemon juice

METHOD

Thoroughly wash the rose petals, then drain on paper towel. Combine the rose petals with 1 cup of the sugar and rub with your hands until they form a paste.

Dissolve the remaining sugar in 450 ml (15 fl oz) water in a large stainless steel saucepan over low heat. Stir in the rose petal mixture and bring to the boil. Boil for 20 minutes, or until the jam (jelly) is thickened but still slightly runny. Stir in the lemon juice, then remove from the heat.

Pour the jam into sterilised jars (see page 185) and seal.

NOTE

Spread the rose petal jam (jelly) on toast, or fold it through plain yoghurt.

MEZE AND SALADS

MEZE IS A MEAL OF LITTLE DISHES, SHARED WITH A GROUP OF FAMILY OR FRIENDS — A TABLE LADEN WITH LOVELY MORSELS SUCH AS WATERMELON, SLICED CUCUMBERS, SLICED TOMATOES, FRIED LIVERS, OLIVES AND FETA.

HUMMUS

INGREDIENTS

250 g (9 oz) dried chickpeas
3 garlic cloves, crushed
80 ml (3 fl oz) tahini
juice of 1 lemon
sea salt
125 ml (4 fl oz) extra-virgin
   olive oil

METHOD

Soak the chickpeas in water for 8 hours. Drain and rinse, then place in a saucepan and cover with cold water. Bring to the boil and cook for 1 hour, or until soft. Drain and rinse well.

Blend the chickpeas, garlic, tahini, lemon juice and salt in a food processor, gradually drizzling in the olive oil. Blend in a little more lemon juice or some hot water if the hummus is too thick.

NOTE

Boiling your own chickpeas will give the hummus a much better texture and flavour than using canned chickpeas.

CAPSICUM DIP

INGREDIENTS

2 red capsicums (peppers)

3 long red chillies

2 tablespoons cumin seeds

2 garlic cloves

125 ml (4 fl oz) extra-virgin
   olive oil

3 tablespoons pomegranate
   molasses (see page 186)

pinch of sea salt

125 g (4 oz) chopped walnuts

METHOD

Cook the capsicums and chillies over a gas burner or barbecue until
the skin is blackened. Put the capsicums and chillies in a plastic bag
to cool, then peel off the skin. Cut the capsicums in half and remove
the seeds.

Stir the cumin seeds in a dry frying pan over medium heat for about
5 minutes, or until fragrant. Use a mortar and pestle to finely grind
the cumin seeds.

Blend the capsicums, chillies, garlic, olive oil, pomegranate molasses,
cumin and sea salt until the mixture forms a smooth paste. Fold the
walnuts through the dip.

BABA GHANOUSH

SERVES FOUR

INGREDIENTS

2 eggplants (aubergines)
sea salt
2 garlic cloves, crushed
3 tablespoons tahini
juice of 1 lemon
80 ml (3 fl oz) extra-virgin
   olive oil

METHOD

Cook the eggplants over a gas burner or barbecue until the skin is blackened and the flesh is soft. Cool slightly, then peel the eggplant and put the flesh in a colander. Sprinkle with sea salt and allow the liquid to drain. Squeeze the excess liquid from the eggplant.

Using a mortar and pestle, grind the eggplant, garlic, tahini and lemon juice. Gradually add the olive oil and grind into a smooth paste.

CARROT DIP

SERVES FOUR

INGREDIENTS

80 g (3 oz) pistachios
3 tablespoons olive oil
300 g (10½ oz) carrots, grated
250 g (9 oz) garlic yoghurt
   (see page 185)
2 tablespoons toasted sesame
   seeds

METHOD

Preheat the oven to 160°C (320°F/Gas 2–3). Spread the pistachios on a baking tray. Roast for 10 minutes, or until fragrant. Crush the cooled pistachios in a food processor.

Heat the olive oil in a frying pan over medium heat. Cook the carrot for 5–6 minutes, or until soft. Set aside to cool.

Fold the carrot through the garlic yoghurt and sprinkle it with the pistachios and sesame seeds.

BEETROOT DIP

SERVES FOUR

INGREDIENTS

2 beetroots (beets)
3 tablespoons dukkah (see
    page 59)
250 g (9 oz) garlic yoghurt
    (see page 185)
extra-virgin olive oil to serve

METHOD

Preheat the oven to 160°C (320°F/Gas 2–3). Wrap the beetroots in foil
and bake for 30 minutes, or until soft. Set aside to cool.

Peel and finely grate the roasted beetroots. Fold the beetroot and
dukkah through the garlic yoghurt. Serve drizzled with extra-virgin
olive oil.

SPINACH DIP

SERVES FOUR

INGREDIENTS

4 handfuls baby English spinach
    leaves, chopped
sea salt
1 onion, diced
3 tablespoons extra-virgin olive oil
250 g (9 oz) garlic yoghurt (see
    page 185)

METHOD

Put the chopped spinach leaves in a non-stick frying pan. Sprinkle
with a little sea salt and stir over low heat until soft. Tip the spinach
into a colander to drain.

Meanwhile, fry the onion in the olive oil in a frying pan over medium
heat for 10–15 minutes, or until very soft but not brown. Squeeze the
excess liquid from the spinach, then add the spinach to the pan with
the onion. Sauté for a few minutes, then sprinkle with a pinch of sea
salt. Set aside to cool, then fold the spinach through the garlic yoghurt.

TURKISH BREAD

MAKES ABOUT TEN LOAVES

INGREDIENTS

4 tablespoons active dry yeast

$\frac{1}{2}$ teaspoon sugar

4 cups plain (all-purpose) flour

1 tablespoon sea salt

3 tablespoons olive oil, plus extra, for rubbing

2 eggs, lightly beaten

40 g ($1\frac{1}{2}$ oz) nigella seeds (see page 186)

40 g ($1\frac{1}{2}$ oz) sesame seeds

When I was growing up, we would take our own paste of ground lamb mince, parsley, garlic, chillies and tomatoes to the local bakery and they would make it into *pide* (Turkish bread) for us.

METHOD

Mix the yeast and sugar with 375 ml ($12\frac{1}{2}$ fl oz) warm water and set aside until the yeast starts foaming, about 5 minutes. Combine the flour and salt in a large bowl. Gradually incorporate the yeast mixture, mixing with your hands, then mix in the olive oil and 125 ml (4 fl oz) warm water. Knead the dough until soft, about 10 minutes. Form the dough into a large ball, rub with olive oil and place in a large bowl. Cover the dough with a tea towel and leave it in a warm place away from draughts for 1 hour, or until doubled in size.

Preheat the oven to at least 250°C (500°F/Gas 9). Dust a baking tray with flour. Take a piece of dough about the size of a golf ball. Roll the dough into a ball and then slightly flatten it. With wet hands, press and knead the dough into a circle. Stretch out the dough until it forms a 25 cm (10 in) circle, and brush it well with some of the beaten egg. Using the side of your hands, press out a border about 3 cm (1 in) wide around the edge of the dough.

Dip your fingers into the beaten egg, point your fingers down to make a claw, and mark out four deep parallel rows, without breaking through the dough. Mark out another four rows, perpendicular to the first four.

Sprinkle a wooden paddle or board with flour and lift the loaf onto it, stretching it out into an oval shape as you pull it onto the paddle. Brush well with the egg and sprinkle nigella seeds and sesame seeds over the top. Repeat with the remaining dough to make 10 loaves.

Slide the dough onto the prepared tray and bake for 8–10 minutes, or until golden. Wrap the *pide* in a clean tea towel and serve hot.

CUCUMBER AND YOGHURT DIP

SERVES FOUR

INGREDIENTS

½ Lebanese (short) cucumber, finely diced
sea salt
2 garlic cloves, crushed
200 g (7 oz) Greek-style plain yoghurt
2 tablespoons mint leaves

METHOD

Put the diced cucumber in a colander, sprinkle with salt and leave to drain for 10 minutes. Squeeze the excess liquid from the cucumber.

Fold the cucumber, garlic and a pinch of salt through the yoghurt. Serve sprinkled with the mint.

VARIATION

For a cold summer soup, stir 500 ml (17 fl oz) water through the dip, drizzle with extra-virgin olive oil and serve with crusty bread.

SPICY TOMATO DIP

SERVES FOUR

INGREDIENTS

250 g (9 oz) onions

250 g (9 oz) tomato paste

1 bunch flat-leaf parsley, finely
chopped

125 g (4 oz) finely chopped green
chillies

250 g (9 oz) tomatoes, seeded and
finely chopped

125 ml (4 fl oz) lemon juice

125 g (4 oz) dried chilli flakes

125 ml (4 fl oz) olive oil

METHOD

Grate the onions and squeeze out the excess liquid.

Mix the onion with the remaining ingredients in a large bowl. Cover
and refrigerate for about 3 hours before serving. Serve as a dip, or with
chicken or lamb.

VARIATION

*Stir through 250 g (9 oz) chopped walnuts or 2 crushed garlic cloves before
serving the dip.*

YOGHURT SEMIZOTU

SERVES FOUR

INGREDIENTS

500 g (1 lb 2 oz) purslane
(pigweed, see page 186)

40 g (1 1/2 oz) butter

3 eggs

500 g (1 lb 2 oz) garlic yoghurt
(see page 185)

flatbread to serve

METHOD

Wash and chop the purslane. Melt the butter in a frying pan over
medium heat. Cook the purslane, stirring, for 3–4 minutes, or until soft.
Gently stir through the eggs until scrambled.

Serve immediately, with the garlic yoghurt and flatbread.

WALNUT AND FETA DIP

SERVES FOUR

INGREDIENTS

125 g (4 oz) chopped walnuts
200 g (7 oz) Bulgarian feta, crumbled
1 small onion, grated
40 g (1$\frac{1}{2}$ oz) butter, at room temperature
3 tablespoons extra-virgin olive oil
freshly cracked black pepper
crusty bread to serve

METHOD

Combine all of the ingredients in a bowl. Serve with crusty bread as a starter or as part of the meze.

ZUCCHINI DIP

SERVES FOUR

INGREDIENTS

3 tablespoons extra-virgin olive oil
1 zucchini (courgette), chopped
125 g (4 oz) garlic yoghurt (see page 185)
1 tablespoon chopped dill

METHOD

Heat the olive oil in a frying pan. Cook the zucchini over high heat for 5 minutes, or until browned. Set aside to cool.

Fold the zucchini through the garlic yoghurt and sprinkle with the dill.

DUKKAH

MAKES ABOUT TWO CUPS

INGREDIENTS
150 g (5 oz) hazelnuts
100 g (3½ oz) sesame seeds
60 g (2 oz) coriander seeds
50 g (2 oz) cumin seeds
1 teaspoon sea salt
½ teaspoon freshly ground
   black pepper

METHOD
Preheat the oven to 160°C (320°F/Gas 2–3). Roast the hazelnuts on a baking tray for 10 minutes, or until fragrant. Rub the hazelnuts in a clean tea towel to remove the skins. Chop in a food processor until the hazelnuts are the size of coarse breadcrumbs.

Stir the sesame seeds, coriander seeds and cumin seeds in a dry frying pan over high heat for 5 minutes, or until fragrant. Transfer the seeds to a mortar and roughly grind with a pestle.

Combine the nuts and seeds with the sea salt and black pepper. Store in an airtight container for up to a month.

NOTE

Serve dukkah sprinkled over dips or Turkish bread.

DOLMADES

INGREDIENTS

500 ml (17 fl oz) olive oil
1 large onion, diced
100 g (3^1/2 oz) pine nuts
2 cups short-grain white rice
1 tomato, diced
100 g (3^1/2 oz) currants
1 handful flat-leaf parsley,
    chopped
^{1}/2 handful chopped dill
sea salt
freshly cracked black pepper
375 g (13 oz) packet vine leaves
    in brine
1 lemon, sliced
garlic yoghurt (see page 185)
    to serve

METHOD

Heat half the olive oil in a frying pan. Cook the onion over medium heat for 10–15 minutes, or until soft but not browned. Add the pine nuts and cook, stirring, until browned. Stir in the rice, tomato, currants and parsley. Add 125 ml (4 fl oz) water and cook, stirring, until just combined. Add the dill and season to taste with sea salt and black pepper. Set aside to cool.

Thoroughly rinse the vine leaves. Place a vine leaf on a flat surface with the rough side facing up. Top with 1 tablespoon of the filling. Fold the top over the filling, fold in the sides, and then roll up like a cigar.

Arrange the lemon slices and any loose stems or broken leaves from the packet of vine leaves over the base of a saucepan. Tightly pack the dolmades in a single layer, then add another layer on top.

Pour the remaining olive oil and 250 ml (8^1/2 fl oz) water over the dolmades and weigh them down with a saucer. Cover and bring to the boil. Reduce the heat to low and cook for 20–25 minutes, or until tender. Set aside to cool in the pan.

Serve the dolmades hot or cold, with garlic yoghurt.

BRAISED GREEN BEANS

SERVES FOUR

INGREDIENTS

1 kg (2 lb 3 oz) young green beans
125 ml (4 fl oz) olive oil
1 large onion, finely diced
2 tomatoes, diced
pinch of sea salt
1 tablespoon sugar

METHOD

Top and tail the beans, then cut them in half.

Heat the oil in a frying pan and fry the onion over medium heat for 10–15 minutes, or until the onion is soft but not browned. Add the beans, tomato, salt and sugar. Cover and cook over low heat for 15 minutes, or until the beans are tender and most of the liquid has evaporated. Add a little water if the mixture is too dry.

Serve the braised beans hot or cold.

NOTE

Refrigerate the beans for up to three days.

FRESH BORLOTTI BEANS WITH TOMATO

SERVES FOUR

INGREDIENTS

250 ml ($8^1/2$ fl oz) olive oil

2 onions, diced

1 kg (2 lb 3 oz) shelled fresh
borlotti beans

500 g (1 lb 2 oz) tomatoes, peeled
and diced (see page 185)

sea salt

freshly cracked black pepper

125 ml (4 fl oz) extra-virgin
olive oil

juice of $^1/2$ lemon

crusty bread to serve

lemon wedges to serve

METHOD

Heat the olive oil in an earthenware pot or heavy-based saucepan. Cook the onion over medium heat for 10–15 minutes, or until soft but not browned.

Add the borlotti beans and tomato to the pan. Season with sea salt and black pepper. Reduce the heat to low, cover and cook for 1 hour, or until the borlotti beans are soft. Stir after 30 minutes, adding a little water or chicken stock if the beans are drying out.

Pour the extra-virgin olive oil and lemon juice over the borlotti beans. Serve hot or cold with crusty bread and lemon wedges.

STUFFED TOMATOES

INGREDIENTS

6–8 very firm vine-ripened
   tomatoes
$1/2$ teaspoon cumin seeds
1 cup long-grain white rice
40 g ($1^1/2$ oz) butter
1 onion, chopped
$1/2$ teaspoon ground allspice
250 g (9 oz) minced (ground)
   lamb
2 handfuls flat-leaf parsley
sea salt
freshly cracked black pepper
185 ml (6 fl oz) beef stock or water
125 ml (4 fl oz) olive oil
80 g (3 oz) unsalted butter
garlic yoghurt (see page 185)
   to serve
crusty bread to serve

METHOD

Slice the tops off the tomatoes. Scoop out and reserve the tomato flesh and seeds.

Use a mortar and pestle to grind the cumin seeds until fine.

Put the rice and 250 ml ($8^1/2$ fl oz) water in a saucepan. Bring to the boil, then reduce the heat and simmer for 10 minutes, or until just tender. Drain.

Melt the butter in a saucepan over medium heat. Sauté the onion until soft but not browned, about 10 minutes. Add the allspice and ground cumin. Stir in the rice and lamb, then add the parsley and season with sea salt and black pepper. Add the beef stock or water and simmer for 8–10 minutes, or until the lamb is just cooked through. Stir in the reserved tomato flesh and seeds.

Spoon the lamb mixture into the tomato shells. Place the tomatoes in a heavy-based frying pan and pour in 250 ml ($8^1/2$ fl oz) hot water and the olive oil. Dot with the butter and sprinkle with sea salt and black pepper. Simmer for 20 minutes, or until the tomatoes are cooked. Serve with garlic yoghurt and crusty bread, or a simple garden salad.

SMOKED EGGPLANT

SERVES FOUR

INGREDIENTS

2 eggplants (aubergines)

sea salt

3 tablespoons lemon juice

2 garlic cloves

1 tomato, diced

1 small red (Spanish) onion,
   diced

1 red chilli, finely chopped

2 handfuls flat-leaf parsley,
   chopped

125 ml (4 fl oz) extra-virgin
   olive oil

freshly cracked black pepper

crusty bread to serve

METHOD

Cook the eggplants over a gas burner or barbecue until the skin is blackened and the flesh is soft. Cool slightly, then peel the eggplant and remove the seeds. Put the flesh in a colander, sprinkle with the sea salt and lemon juice and allow the liquid to drain for 20 minutes. Squeeze the excess liquid from the eggplant and transfer the flesh to a bowl.

Using a mortar and pestle, grind the garlic with a little sea salt, then add to the eggplant.

Add the tomato, onion, chilli and parsley to the eggplant. Stir in the olive oil and season to taste with sea salt and black pepper. Serve with crusty bread.

BRAISED BROAD BEANS WITH GARLIC YOGHURT

SERVES FOUR

INGREDIENTS

125 ml (4 fl oz) olive oil

1 large onion, diced

1.5 kg (3 lb 5 oz) broad (fava)
  beans, podded and peeled

sea salt

250 g (9 oz) garlic yoghurt
  (see page 185)

dill sprigs to serve

extra-virgin olive oil to serve

crusty bread to serve

METHOD

Heat the olive oil in a frying pan. Cook the onion over medium heat for 10–15 minutes, or until the onion is soft but not browned. Add the broad beans and season with the sea salt. Cover and simmer for 5–10 minutes, or until the beans are tender. Remove from the heat and transfer to a serving bowl.

Spoon the garlic yoghurt over the broad beans. Sprinkle with the dill sprigs and drizzle with a little extra-virgin olive oil. Serve warm or cold, with crusty bread.

OKRA

INGREDIENTS

1 kg (2 lb 3 oz) small okra
80 g (3 oz) butter
2 onions, diced
2 ripe tomatoes, diced
2 green chillies, chopped
sea salt
freshly cracked black pepper
juice of 1 lemon

METHOD

Trim off the top of the okra and place it in a bowl of water.

Melt the butter in a frying pan over medium heat. Cook the onion for 10–15 minutes, or until soft but not browned. Add the tomato, chilli, okra and 125 ml (4 fl oz) water. Season with sea salt and black pepper and simmer for 5–10 minutes, or until the okra is tender. Stir in the lemon juice.

Serve the okra hot or cold.

NOTE

This is delicious with braised lamb or chicken.

FETA KOFTES

INGREDIENTS

250 g (9 oz) Bulgarian feta
100 g (3½ oz) dried breadcrumbs
2 eggs
½ bunch flat-leaf parsley, chopped
freshly cracked black pepper
sunflower or canola oil, for
    shallow-frying

METHOD

Combine the feta, breadcrumbs, eggs, parsley and pepper in a large bowl. Mix well, then form the mixture into small balls.

Heat the oil in a heavy-based frying pan. Fry the koftes over high heat for 2–3 minutes, or until golden. Drain on paper towels. Serve hot.

PAN-FRIED FETA AND PARSLEY BREADS

MAKES TWELVE

INGREDIENTS

Dough
1 tablespoon active dry yeast
1 tablespoon sugar
2 cups plain (all-purpose) flour
pinch of sea salt

300 g (10½ oz) Bulgarian feta,
    crumbled
2 large handfuls flat-leaf parsley,
    chopped
sunflower or canola oil, for
    shallow-frying

METHOD

To make the dough, mix the yeast and sugar with 80 ml (3 fl oz) warm water and set aside until the yeast starts foaming, about 5 minutes. Combine the flour and salt in a large bowl. Gradually stir in the yeast mixture and about 250 ml (8½ fl oz) warm water to form a soft dough. Knead the dough on a floured board for 10 minutes. The dough should feel like your earlobe. Leave the dough in a warm place for 45 minutes, or until it has doubled in size.

Divide the dough into 12 balls and set aside for 15 minutes. Press each ball into a 12 cm (4¾ in) circle. Combine the feta and chopped parsley and place 2 tablespoons of the filling on one half of each circle. Fold over the dough to make a semicircle and gently press to seal the edges.

Heat the oil in a frying pan and cook the breads over medium heat until brown, about 3–4 minutes. Flip over and brown the other side. Drain on paper towels and serve hot.

BURGHUL SALAD

INGREDIENTS

2 cups fine burghul (bulgar wheat)
3 tomatoes, finely chopped
4 spring onions (scallions),
   chopped
1 red (Spanish) onion, chopped
1 handful mint, chopped
1 handful flat-leaf parsley, chopped
1 tablespoon tomato paste
1 teaspoon dried chilli flakes
1 teaspoon ground cumin
80 ml (3 fl oz) olive oil
juice of ½ lemon
lettuce leaves to serve
lemon wedges to serve

METHOD

Mix the burghul and 375 ml (12½ fl oz) boiling water in a bowl. Set aside for 20 minutes, or until all the water has been absorbed.

Add the remaining ingredients to the burghul and mix to combine. Serve on a platter with the lettuce leaves and lemon wedges.

Groups of women in Turkey get together at one another's houses once a month. The woman hosting the gathering prepares the food and everyone brings a small donation. Most people in Turkey are not wealthy, so it's a way of helping each other out with the bills, while enjoying a meal and talking together.

CURED SALMON WITH DILL

SERVES TEN

INGREDIENTS

1.5 kg (3 lb 5 oz) salmon fillet,
  pin-boned
300 g (10½ oz) rock salt
200 g (7 oz) caster (superfine)
  sugar
1 bunch dill, finely chopped
extra-virgin olive oil to serve
crusty bread to serve

METHOD

Pat the salmon dry with paper towel. Combine the salt and sugar and place a little in the base of a large glass or ceramic dish. Press the dill onto the salmon. Place the salmon on top of the salt and sugar in the dish, then top with the remaining salt and sugar so that the whole fillet is covered.

Place a couple of plates on top of the salmon to weigh it down, cover with plastic wrap (cling film) and refrigerate for 12 hours. Turn the salmon over, replace the plates and refrigerate for another 12 hours.

To serve, scrape the salt and sugar off the salmon and gently rinse it with cold water, leaving the dill on the salmon. Rub the salmon with the extra-virgin olive oil and slice paper-thin slices off the fillet. Serve with crusty bread.

NOTE

This is delicious with zucchini (courgette) fritters (page 135), fennel salad or a simple green salad. Refrigerate the cured salmon for up to 2 weeks.

ALBANIAN FRIED LIVER

SERVES FOUR

INGREDIENTS

1 lamb's liver
$^1/_2$ cup cornflour (cornstarch)
1 tablespoon cayenne pepper
1 tablespoon sea salt
250 ml ($8^1/_2$ fl oz) olive oil

METHOD

Skin and clean the liver and cut it into 1 cm square pieces.

Combine the cornflour, cayenne pepper and sea salt in a bowl.

Heat the olive oil in a frying pan over high heat. Toss the liver in the cornflour mixture and fry in small batches for 5 minutes each batch, or until golden. Serve the liver hot or cold as part of the meze.

BEETROOT AND FETA SALAD

SERVES FOUR

INGREDIENTS

2 beetroots (beets)

250 g (9 oz) pumpkin, cut into 2 cm (³/₄ in) cubes

2 large handfuls rocket (arugula)

1 small red (Spanish) onion, sliced

2 ripe tomatoes, diced

100 g (3¹/₂ oz) Bulgarian feta

2 heaped tablespoons dukkah (see page 59)

Dressing

3 tablespoons pomegranate molasses (see page 186)

2 tablespoons extra-virgin olive oil

METHOD

Preheat the oven to 160°C (320°F/Gas 2–3). Wrap the beetroots in foil and bake for 20 minutes, then add the pumpkin and cook for another 20 minutes, or until the beetroot is soft and the pumpkin is golden. Set aside to cool. Peel and chop the cooled beetroots.

To make the dressing, whisk the pomegranate molasses with the olive oil until combined.

Put the rocket in a serving bowl and top with the beetroot, pumpkin, onion and tomato. Drizzle with the dressing, then crumble the feta over the salad. Sprinkle with the dukkah to serve.

SMOKED EGGPLANT SALAD

SERVES FOUR

INGREDIENTS

2 small eggplants (aubergines)
1 large handful flat-leaf parsley,
    chopped
1 tomato, diced
1 small red (Spanish) onion, diced
2 garlic cloves, crushed
1 green chilli, finely chopped
125 ml (4 fl oz) extra-virgin
    olive oil
juice of 1 lemon
sea salt
freshly cracked black pepper
crusty bread to serve

METHOD

Cook the eggplants over a gas burner or barbecue until the skin is blackened and the flesh is soft. Cool slightly, then peel the eggplant and chop the flesh.

Combine the eggplant with the remaining ingredients. Serve at room temperature with crusty bread.

PARSLEY SALAD WITH LEMON JUICE

SERVES FOUR

INGREDIENTS

1 red (Spanish) onion
2 tablespoons lemon juice
2 tablespoons sumac (see page 187)
pinch of sea salt
2 handfuls flat-leaf parsley, chopped

METHOD

Cut the onion in half lengthwise and then into thin slices.

Sprinkle the onion with the lemon juice, sumac and sea salt and mix with your hands, rubbing together. Mix in the parsley, and serve.

NOTE

I love to serve this with barbecued chicken, chargrilled tomatoes and green capsicums (peppers), flatbread and fresh mint. It is also good with barbecued meat or fish.

SHEPHERD'S SALAD

SERVES FOUR

INGREDIENTS

500 g (1 lb 2 oz) vine-ripened
    tomatoes
1 Lebanese (short) cucumber
1 red (Spanish) onion
2 long green chillies
$1/2$ bunch flat-leaf parsley
100 ml ($3^1/2$ fl oz) olive oil
juice of 1 lemon
sea salt
freshly cracked black pepper

METHOD

Cut the tomatoes, cucumber and onion into 2 cm ($3/4$ in) squares and place in a large bowl. Thickly slice the chillies and add to the bowl.

Add the parsley, olive oil and lemon juice and toss to combine. Season to taste with sea salt and black pepper.

TURMERIC AND CHILLI CHICKEN IN FLATBREAD

SERVES FOUR

INGREDIENTS

1 kg (2 lb 3 oz) chicken thighs,
 cut into bite-sized pieces
2 tablespoons ground turmeric
2 tablespoons dried chilli flakes
sea salt
3 tablespoons cumin seeds
250 g (9 oz) garlic yoghurt
 (see page 185)
2 handfuls mint leaves
2 handfuls coriander (cilantro)
 leaves
1 bunch flat-leaf parsley
3 tomatoes, diced
1 red (Spanish) onion, sliced
3 green chillies, diced
freshly cracked black pepper
3 tablespoons pomegranate seeds
3 tablespoons olive oil
flatbread to serve

METHOD

Combine the chicken with the turmeric, chilli flakes and a pinch of sea salt and marinate in the refrigerator for 2 hours.

Stir the cumin seeds in a dry frying pan over high heat until fragrant.

Put the cumin seeds, garlic yoghurt, mint leaves, coriander leaves, parsley, tomato, onion, chilli, sea salt and black pepper in separate bowls. Sprinkle the pomegranate seeds over the parsley.

Heat the olive oil in a frying pan and cook the chicken over high heat for 10–15 minutes, or until cooked through. Transfer the chicken to a bowl.

Grill the flatbread until warmed through.

Serve all the bowls in the centre of the table. Put a little of each ingredient into the warm bread and eat, while the juices run down your arms.

BEAN PURÉE

INGREDIENTS

100 g (3^1/$_2$ oz) dried lima beans
250 ml (8^1/$_2$ fl oz) olive oil
125 ml (4 fl oz) lemon juice
1 onion
50 g (2 oz) English mustard
^{1}/$_2$ teaspoon chilli powder

METHOD

Soak the lima beans in water for 5 hours. Drain and rinse, then place in a saucepan and cover with cold water. Bring to the boil and cook for 1 hour, or until tender. Drain and rinse well.

Put the beans in a food processor, add the remaining ingredients and blend to a thick purée.

EGGPLANT WITH GARLIC YOGHURT

SERVES FOUR

INGREDIENTS

2 eggplants (aubergines)
sea salt
2 garlic cloves
500 g (1 lb 2 oz) Greek-style
  plain yoghurt
3 tablespoons extra-virgin
  olive oil
pinch of sweet paprika
crusty bread to serve

METHOD

Cook the eggplants over a gas burner or barbecue until the skin is blackened and the flesh is soft. Cool slightly, then peel the eggplant and put the flesh in a colander. Sprinkle with sea salt and allow the liquid to drain, then roughly chop the eggplant.

Using a mortar and pestle, crush the garlic with a pinch of sea salt. Fold the garlic through the yoghurt, then fold the eggplant through the yoghurt. Serve drizzled with the extra-virgin olive oil, paprika and crusty bread.

CHICKPEA AND FETA SALAD WITH CHILLI AND DUKKAH

SERVES FOUR

INGREDIENTS

250 g (9 oz) dried chickpeas
125 ml (4 fl oz) extra-virgin
    olive oil
juice of 1 lemon
2 tomatoes, diced
1 red (Spanish) onion, diced
1 red chilli, chopped
2 handfuls flat-leaf parsley
sea salt
freshly cracked black pepper
150 g (5 oz) Bulgarian feta,
    crumbled
2 tablespoons dukkah (see
    page 59)

METHOD

Soak the chickpeas in water for 8 hours. Drain and rinse, then place in a saucepan and cover with cold water. Bring to the boil and cook for 1 hour, or until soft. Drain and rinse well.

Combine the extra-virgin olive oil and lemon juice in a large bowl. Add the tomato, onion, chilli, parsley and season with sea salt and black pepper. Mix the chickpeas through the salad. Add the feta, sprinkle with the dukkah and serve at room temperature.

NOTES

You can use a 400 g (14 oz) can of chickpeas instead of the dried chickpeas. They will not need to be cooked.

Sometimes I add farro to this recipe. Farro is grown among wheat and looks like wheat. It has a nutty, chewy texture and is a beautiful addition wherever you might normally add rice. Dry-fry 200 g (7 oz) farro, then add 250 ml (8½ fl oz) water and a pinch of salt. Reduce the heat and gently cook for 30 minutes. Add some roasted pumpkin and toss the farro and pumpkin through the salad.

MAIN MEALS

FAMILIES IN TURKEY NORMALLY EAT AT HOME. IT'S A TIME WHEN WE SHARE. THE WOMEN SPEND THE DAY PREPARING THE FOOD, AND AT DINNERTIME PEOPLE COME TOGETHER TO TALK AND EAT FOR HOURS.

CHARGRILLED CHICKEN WITH GREEN CHILLIES AND TOMATO

SERVES FOUR

INGREDIENTS

500 g (1 lb 2 oz) chicken thighs
3 tablespoons olive oil
juice of 1 lemon
sea salt
freshly cracked black pepper
4 tomatoes
4 long green chillies
flatbread to serve

Sumac and parsley salad
1 red (Spanish) onion,
   thinly sliced
2 tablespoons sumac
   (see page 187)
2 handfuls flat-leaf parsley,
   chopped

METHOD

Mix the chicken with the olive oil and lemon juice in a bowl and season with sea salt and black pepper. Cover and marinate in the refrigerator for 1 hour.

To make the sumac and parsley salad, sprinkle the onion with the sumac and parsley. Using your hands, crush the ingredients together.

Cut the tomatoes into wedges and sprinkle with sea salt. Chargrill the chicken on a barbecue for 5–10 minutes, or until browned and cooked through. Cook the tomatoes and chillies until soft.

Arrange the chicken, chillies and tomatoes on a platter. Invite your guests to fill the flatbread with the chicken, chillies, tomatoes and sumac and parsley salad.

NOTE

You can also pan-fry the chicken, tomatoes and chillies in olive oil.

MUSSELS WITH WALNUT TARATOR

SERVES FOUR

INGREDIENTS

36 large mussels
375 ml (12½ fl oz) beer
½ cup plain (all-purpose) flour,
    plus extra, for dusting
pinch of sea salt
sunflower or canola oil, for
    deep-frying
lemon wedges to serve

Tarator
150 g (5 oz) walnuts
2 garlic cloves, crushed
100 g (3½ oz) dried breadcrumbs
3 tablespoons olive oil
pinch of sea salt
80 ml (3 fl oz) lemon juice

METHOD

Scrub the mussels and remove the beards. Discard any open mussels that do not close when tapped on a hard surface.

To make the tarator, use a mortar and pestle to grind the walnuts with the garlic. Add the breadcrumbs and about 3 tablespoons of water to moisten. Mix in the olive oil, sea salt and lemon juice to give a creamy consistency. Set aside while you cook the mussels.

Gradually stir the beer into the combined flour and salt to make a smooth batter. Open the mussel shells and remove the flesh. Toss the mussels in the extra flour, and then toss them into the batter.

Heat the oil in a deep heavy-based saucepan to about 180°C (350°F). Lower the mussels, in batches, into the hot oil and cook until golden, about 30 seconds. If you overcook the mussels they will be tough. Drain the mussels on paper towel.

Serve the mussels immediately. Spoon the tarator onto serving plates, then top with the mussels and a wedge of lemon.

NOTE

Tarator makes a beautiful sauce for chicken or any seafood.

BROWN LENTIL AND ONION SOUP

SERVES FOUR

INGREDIENTS

200 g (7 oz) brown lentils
125 ml (4 fl oz) olive oil
1 onion, diced
2 litres (68 fl oz) chicken or
  vegetable stock
sea salt
freshly cracked black pepper
1 tablespoon plain (all-purpose)
  flour
60 g (2 oz) butter
2 onions, extra, sliced
croutons to serve

METHOD

Put the lentils in a saucepan and cover with plenty of water. Bring to the boil and cook for 20 minutes, or until the lentils are just tender. Drain and set aside.

Heat the olive oil in a large saucepan and fry the diced onion over medium heat for 10–15 minutes, or until soft but not browned. Add the lentils and stock and season to taste with sea salt and black pepper. Cook for 15–20 minutes, or until the lentils are soft.

Mix a little of the liquid with the flour, then add it to the soup, stirring constantly until thickened, about 5 minutes.

Melt the butter in a frying pan over high heat. Cook the sliced onion, stirring, for 5–10 minutes, until the onion is caramelised.

To serve, sprinkle the hot soup with the croutons and then spoon the onion over the top.

VARIATION

This is also delicious sprinkled with crushed roasted hazelnuts.

YAMBA PRAWNS

SERVES FOUR

INGREDIENTS

12 raw prawns (shrimps)
200 g (7 oz) pappardelle
125 ml (4 fl oz) extra-virgin
  olive oil
6 garlic cloves, finely chopped
3 red chillies, finely chopped
sea salt
2 handfuls flat-leaf parsley,
  chopped
lemon wedges to serve

METHOD

Peel and devein the prawns, leaving the tails on.

Cook the pasta in a large saucepan of boiling salted water until al dente, then drain.

Meanwhile, heat the olive oil in a large frying pan. Fry the garlic and chilli over medium heat for 10 minutes, or until soft but not browned. Add the prawns and cook over high heat for 2 minutes on one side, then sprinkle with sea salt. Turn the prawns, add the pasta and parsley and sprinkle with a little more salt. Toss until the pasta has warmed through. Serve with lemon wedges.

VARIATION

This recipe also works well with pipis.

CHICKEN LIVERS WITH CARAMELISED ONION

SERVES TWO

INGREDIENTS

Caramelised onion
4 large onions
80 ml (3 fl oz) canola oil or
    light olive oil
sea salt
1 tablespoon balsamic vinegar

canola oil, for cooking
300 g (10½ oz) chicken livers
sea salt
1 heaped tablespoon freshly
    ground black pepper
1 bunch rocket (arugula)
2 tomatoes, cut into wedges
2 tablespoons dukkah (see
    page 59)

METHOD

To make the caramelised onion, cut the onions in half lengthwise and then into slices. Put the oil and onion in a heavy-based frying pan just large enough to hold the onion. Sprinkle with sea salt and slowly cook over medium heat for 30 minutes, occasionally scraping the bottom of the pan. Add the balsamic vinegar and cook for another 30 minutes, or until the onions are flecked with brown but not too dark. Take care not to burn them.

Add enough canola oil to a medium frying pan to cover the base of the pan. Heat the oil, add the chicken livers and sprinkle with the sea salt and black pepper. Cook over high heat for 1½–2 minutes each side, being careful not to overcook the livers. They should be brown on the outside and just pink in the middle.

Add the caramelised onion to the pan and cook, gently turning the onion, until heated through.

Arrange the rocket and tomato in the centre of two serving plates. Spoon the livers on top of the salad, then spoon over the remainder of the caramelised onion and sprinkle with the dukkah.

CORN FRITTERS WITH POLENTA

SERVES FOUR

INGREDIENTS

1 corn cob
1 onion, diced
$^1/_2$ cup polenta
4 handfuls flat-leaf parsley,
    chopped
2 eggs
1 tablespoon baking powder
sea salt
freshly cracked black pepper
250 ml ($8^1/_2$ fl oz) sunflower or
    canola oil

METHOD

Cut the kernels off the corn cob and place in a bowl. Add the onion, polenta, parsley, eggs and baking powder and season with sea salt and black pepper. Stir for a few minutes, until the batter is well combined.

Heat the oil in a frying pan over high heat. Drop 2 tablespoons of the batter at a time into the hot oil and cook for 3–4 minutes on each side, or until golden. Drain on paper towels. Serve hot or cold.

LAMB KOFTE

SERVES FOUR

INGREDIENTS

Tomato sauce

3 tablespoons olive oil

1 onion, roughly chopped

3 garlic cloves

500 g (1 lb 2 oz) canned crushed
    tomatoes

2 teaspoons sugar

sea salt

freshly cracked black pepper

3 tablespoons cumin seeds

1 kg (2 lb 3 oz) minced (ground)
    lamb

1 large brown onion, grated

4 handfuls flat-leaf parsley,
    chopped

2 tablespoons baharat (see
    page 186)

sea salt

freshly cracked black pepper

125 ml (4 fl oz) sunflower or
    canola oil

2 handfuls flat-leaf parsley, extra,
    chopped

garlic yoghurt (see page 185)
    to serve

METHOD

To make the tomato sauce, heat the olive oil in a large saucepan. Gently fry the onion over medium heat for 10–15 minutes, or until soft but not browned. Add the whole garlic cloves and fry for 2 minutes more. Pour in the tomato and cook for 30 minutes, or until the mixture has thickened. Stir in the sugar halfway through cooking. Season to taste with sea salt and black pepper. Cool slightly, then purée until smooth.

Fry the cumin seeds in a dry frying pan over high heat for 5 minutes, or until fragrant. Transfer the seeds to a mortar and finely grind with a pestle.

Put the minced lamb in a large bowl. Add the onion, parsley, baharat and cumin and season with sea salt and black pepper. Mix with your hands until well combined.

Roll 1 tablespoon of the lamb mixture into an oval shape between the palms of your hands. Heat the oil in a frying pan and cook the kofte over high heat for 2 minutes each side, or until just firm. Taste, then adjust the seasoning if necessary. Roll the remaining lamb mixture into balls and fry until just firm. Drain on paper towel.

Serve with the parsley, tomato sauce, garlic yoghurt and a simple salad.

> **NOTE**
>
> *You can also barbecue the kofte, or bake them in a 180°C (350°F/Gas 4) oven for 8 minutes.*

ROASTED CAPSICUM AND CORIANDER SOUP

SERVES FOUR

INGREDIENTS

3 red capsicums (peppers)
1 bunch coriander (cilantro)
125 ml (4 fl oz) extra-virgin
   olive oil
1 onion, diced
3 garlic cloves
500 ml (17 fl oz) chicken or
   vegetable stock
500 g (1 lb 2 oz) tomatoes, diced
1 red chilli, finely chopped
sea salt
freshly cracked black pepper
250 g (9 oz) canned chickpeas,
   optional
croutons to serve

METHOD

Cook the capsicums over a gas burner or barbecue until the skin is blackened. Put the capsicums in a plastic bag to cool, then peel off the skin. Remove the seeds and dice the flesh.

Chop the coriander roots and reserve the leaves for garnishing.

Heat the olive oil in a large saucepan. Fry the onion and garlic over medium heat for 10 minutes, or until soft but not browned. Add the stock, tomato, capsicum, chilli and coriander roots. Season to taste with sea salt and black pepper and cook for 20–30 minutes, or until the vegetables are tender.

Cool slightly, then purée the soup until smooth. Add the drained chickpeas, if using, and stir over low heat until warmed through.

Serve the soup garnished with the coriander leaves and croutons.

SEVTAP'S TURKISH CHICKEN

INGREDIENTS

1 kg (2 lb 3 oz) chicken thighs
3 tablespoons olive oil
1 large onion, chopped
1 tablespoon ground allspice
3 cinnamon sticks
1 kg (2 lb 3 oz) tomatoes, diced
3 long green chillies
100 g (3½ oz) pine nuts, toasted
100 g (3½ oz) currants
2 handfuls flat-leaf parsley
sea salt
freshly cracked black pepper

METHOD

Cut the chicken thighs into bite-sized pieces.

Heat the olive oil in a large saucepan. Fry the onion over medium heat for 10–15 minutes, or until soft but not browned. Add the chicken, allspice and cinnamon sticks and stir to coat the chicken. Add the tomato, chillies, pine nuts, currants and parsley. Sprinkle with a little salt and lots of black pepper. Cover and cook over low heat for 40 minutes, or until the chicken is tender.

NOTE

Serve the chicken with rice pilaf (see page 114), cucumber, red (Spanish) onion, coriander (cilantro) leaves and mint leaves. Traditionally the rice is cooked with the spices, pine nuts and currants, but I prefer to cook them with the chicken.

RICE PILAF

INGREDIENTS

1 cup short-grain rice
375 ml (12$\frac{1}{2}$ fl oz) chicken stock
    or water
80 g (3 oz) butter
1 brown onion, diced
sea salt
2 tablespoons pine nuts
2 tablespoons currants
2 tablespoons chopped flat-leaf
    parsley

METHOD

Rinse the rice under cold running water, then set aside to drain.

Heat the stock or water in a small saucepan.

Melt the butter in a heavy-based saucepan over medium heat. Add the onion and sauté for 10–15 minutes, or until soft but not browned. Add the rice and cook, gently stirring, for 5 minutes.

Add the hot stock or water to the rice and season with sea salt. Cook over low heat for 10 minutes, or until almost all of the liquid has been absorbed. Reduce the heat, cover and steam the rice for 15 minutes.

Remove the rice from the heat and let it stand, covered, for another 15 minutes.

Meanwhile, fry the pine nuts in a dry frying pan over high heat for 3–5 minutes, or until golden. Combine with the currants.

Gently stir the rice to separate the grains, and serve sprinkled with the pine nuts, currants and parsley.

VARIATIONS

I like this dish served on its own, or with braised lima beans (see page 126), pickled vegetables and green salad on the side. Alternatively, sprinkle the pilaf with chilli and flat-leaf parsley, or serve with pan-fried chicken thighs, onion, pine nuts, currants and flat-leaf parsley.

This was my brother Murat's favourite dish. When we were children he loved to eat pilaf for dinner, as a simple meal served with pickled vegetables, smashed onion and braised white beans.

CHICKEN KOFTE

SERVES FOUR

INGREDIENTS

1 kg (2 lb 3 oz) minced (ground)
  chicken

1 large onion, finely diced

2 handfuls flat-leaf parsley,
  chopped

4 tablespoons dukkah (see
  page 59)

2 tablespoons chilli flakes

sea salt

freshly cracked black pepper

METHOD

Put the minced chicken in a large bowl. Add the diced onion, parsley, dukkah and chilli flakes. Season with sea salt and black pepper. Using your hands, mix until well combined. Refrigerate for several hours or overnight to allow the flavours to develop.

Roll walnut-sized pieces of the chicken mixture into balls and gently flatten them. Cook the kofte on a preheated barbecue over high heat for 2–3 minutes on each side, or until golden. Drain on paper towels. Serve hot.

NOTE

Chicken kofte are delicious with sumac and parsley salad (see page 96). They can also be pan-fried in a little oil.

FRIED SHEEP'S TESTICLES

SERVES FOUR

INGREDIENTS

6 sheep's testicles
$1/2$ cup plain (all-purpose) flour
sea salt
2 eggs, beaten
250 ml ($8^{1}/_{2}$ fl oz) olive oil

METHOD

Cut the testicles in half. Put the flour in a bowl and season with sea salt. Put the beaten eggs in another bowl. Dip the testicles into the flour and then into the beaten eggs.

Heat the olive oil in a heavy-based frying pan, then fry the testicles over high heat until golden brown, about 2–3 minutes on each side. Serve hot.

NOTE

You can also barbecue the testicles for 3–4 minutes on each side.

CELERIAC SOUP

INGREDIENTS

1 head celeriac

juice of $\frac{1}{2}$ lemon

125 ml (4 fl oz) olive oil

1 large onion, finely diced

3 garlic cloves

2 carrots, diced

3 tomatoes, diced

1 litre (34 fl oz) chicken or
   vegetable stock

2 teaspoons sugar

sea salt

freshly cracked black pepper

2 handfuls flat-leaf parsley,
   chopped

juice of 1 lemon, extra, to serve

METHOD

Peel and dice the celeriac, and toss with the lemon juice.

Heat the olive oil in a large saucepan. Fry the onion and garlic over medium heat for 10–15 minutes, or until soft but not browned. Add the carrot and stir for 2–3 minutes, then add the celeriac, tomato, stock and sugar. Season to taste with sea salt and black pepper. Cover and simmer until the vegetables are tender, about 20 minutes.

Sprinkle with the parsley and extra lemon juice. Serve hot or cold.

NOTES

Refrigerate the soup for up to 3 days.

You can use this recipe to make braised celeriac. Simply cook as above, but omit the stock.

TURKISH-STYLE SARDINES WITH TOMATO SALAD

SERVES FOUR

INGREDIENTS

12 sardines, cleaned

3 tablespoons sunflower oil

2 vine-ripened tomatoes, diced

1 small red (Spanish) onion, diced

2 handfuls flat-leaf parsley,
   roughly chopped

125 ml (4 fl oz) extra-virgin
   olive oil

juice of 1 lemon

sea salt

lemon wedges to serve

METHOD

Remove the heads from the sardines. Wash thoroughly, then drain on paper towel.

Heat the sunflower oil in a non-stick frying pan. Cook the sardines for 2 minutes on each side over high heat, or until golden.

Put the tomato, onion, parsley, olive oil and lemon juice in a bowl and gently toss to combine. Season with sea salt.

Divide the salad between four plates and arrange the sardines on top. Serve with lemon wedges.

EGGPLANT WITH BRAISED BEEF

SERVES FOUR

INGREDIENTS

125 ml (4 fl oz) olive oil
2 brown onions, diced
1 kg (2 lb 3 oz) diced beef
1 kg (2 lb 3 oz) tomatoes, diced
2 tablespoons tomato paste
3 green chillies, chopped
sea salt
freshly cracked black pepper
2 eggplants (aubergines)
125 ml (4 fl oz) sunflower or
   canola oil
2 handfuls flat-leaf parsley,
   chopped
2 handfuls mint leaves
extra-virgin olive oil to serve
garlic yoghurt (see page 185)
   to serve
paprika to serve
Turkish bread to serve

METHOD

Heat the oil in a large saucepan and fry the onion over medium heat for 10–15 minutes, or until soft but not browned. Add the beef and cook until it begins to turn brown. Stir in the tomato, tomato paste and chilli, then season with the sea salt and black pepper. Braise for 1½ hours, or until the beef is tender. Add a little beef stock or water if the mixture starts to dry out during cooking.

Meanwhile, peel the eggplants in strips, then cut into thick slices. Heat the oil in a frying pan and fry the eggplant over high heat for 4–6 minutes, until soft. Transfer the eggplant to an ovenproof dish.

Preheat the oven to 160°C (320°F/Gas 2–3). Stir the parsley into the beef mixture. Sprinkle the eggplant with sea salt and pile the beef on top of the eggplant slices. Bake for 10 minutes, or until the eggplant is heated through. Sprinkle with the mint and drizzle with extra-virgin olive oil. Serve with the garlic yoghurt, paprika and Turkish bread.

VARIATION

Try slicing the eggplants in half lengthwise instead of into rounds. They will take a little longer to cook. The beef is also delicious with couscous, garlic yoghurt and fresh mint and coriander instead of the eggplant.

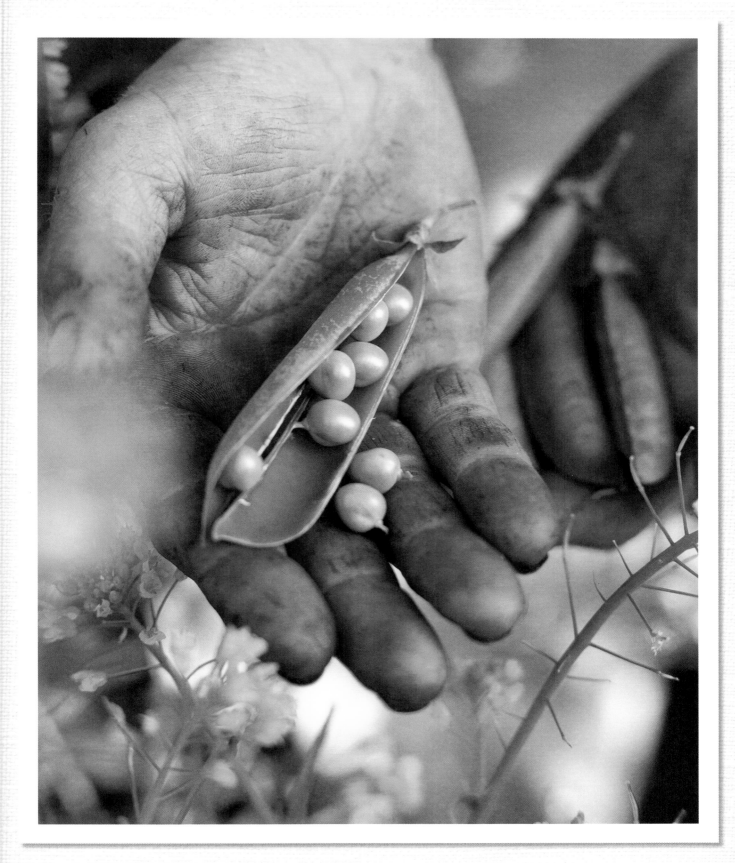

BRAISED LIMA BEANS

SERVES FOUR

INGREDIENTS

250 g (9 oz) dried lima beans

125 ml (4 fl oz) extra-virgin
  olive oil

1 large onion, diced

300 g ($10^1/_2$ oz) tomatoes,
  finely diced

sea salt

freshly cracked black pepper

3 tablespoons extra-virgin olive
  oil, extra, to serve

METHOD

Soak the lima beans overnight in cold water. Drain and rinse the beans, place in a saucepan and cover with plenty of water. Bring to the boil and cook for 1–1$^1/_2$ hours, or until the beans are soft. Drain and set aside.

Heat the olive oil in a saucepan and gently sauté the onion over low heat until soft, about 10 minutes. Add the tomatoes and drained lima beans and cook over low heat for about 1 hour, or until thickened. If the mixture becomes dry, add a little stock or water. Season to taste with sea salt and black pepper. Stir in the extra olive oil to serve.

IMAM BAYILDI

SERVES SIX

INGREDIENTS

6 eggplants (aubergines)
6 garlic cloves, finely sliced
250 ml (8¹/₂ fl oz) olive oil
2 onions, finely diced
6 tomatoes, chopped
1 green capsicum (pepper),
    finely diced
2 handfuls flat-leaf parsley,
    chopped
sea salt
freshly cracked black pepper
garlic yoghurt (see page 185)
    to serve (optional)

METHOD

Preheat the oven to 160°C (320°F/Gas 2–3). Trim the tops off the eggplants and peel them in 1 cm (¹/₂ in) wide strips to give a striped appearance. Cut the eggplants in half lengthwise and push the garlic slices into them. Heat half the oil in a frying pan. Cook the eggplants over high heat, turning, until lightly browned. Remove from the pan.

Heat the remaining olive oil and fry the onion over medium heat for 10–15 minutes, or until soft but not browned. Add the tomato, capsicum and half the parsley, and season with sea salt and black pepper. Cook for another 5 minutes.

Place the eggplants in an ovenproof dish, and make a cut in the centre for the filling. Spoon the tomato mixture into the eggplants. Bake for 40 minutes, or until the eggplants are tender.

Sprinkle the eggplants with the remaining parsley. Serve hot or cold, with garlic yoghurt if you like.

NOTE

Literally translated, 'imam bayildi' means 'The priest fainted'. Some say he fainted because it was the loveliest dish he had ever tasted; some say he fainted because of the amount of expensive olive oil it contains.

SPATCHCOCK WITH PEAS

SERVES FOUR

INGREDIENTS

2 spatchcocks
1 red capsicum (pepper)
250 ml (8½ fl oz) extra-virgin
   olive oil
2 onions, sliced
4 French shallots (small red
   onions), halved
1 kg (2 lb 3 oz) tomatoes, peeled
   and diced
200 g (7 oz) shelled fresh peas
500 g (1 lb 2 oz) potatoes, peeled
   and quartered
3 red chillies
3 garlic cloves
sea salt
freshly cracked black pepper
1 handful flat-leaf parsley
Turkish bread to serve

METHOD

Ask your butcher to cut each spatchcock into 2 leg quarters and 2 breast quarters, leaving the wings attached.

Cook the capsicum over a gas burner or barbecue until the skin is blackened. Put the capsicum in a plastic bag to cool, then peel off the skin. Remove the seeds and chop the flesh.

Heat the olive oil in a frying pan and cook the onion and shallots over medium heat for 10–15 minutes, or until soft but not browned. Add the spatchcock pieces and cook until golden. Remove the breast quarters and set aside.

Add the capsicum and tomato to the pan and cook for 10 minutes. Add the peas, potato, whole chillies and garlic.

Place the breast quarters on top of the vegetables. Cover and cook for 20 minutes, or until the spatchcock is cooked through. Season to taste with sea salt and black pepper.

Serve with the parsley and hot crusty Turkish bread.

NOTE

I like to use whole kipfler potatoes for this dish. They don't need to be peeled.

GARLIC CHILLI SQUID WITH SAFFRON

INGREDIENTS

300 g (10½ oz) cleaned squid

3 tablespoons sunflower oil

3 garlic cloves, chopped

1 red chilli, finely chopped

1 handful flat-leaf parsley, chopped

½ teaspoon saffron threads

sea salt

1 handful rocket (arugula)

100 ml (3½ fl oz) extra-virgin olive oil

juice of 1 lemon

METHOD

Cut the squid into bite-sized pieces.

Heat the sunflower oil in a frying pan until very hot. Cook the squid in the hot oil for 1–2 minutes, or until opaque. Add the garlic, chilli, parsley and saffron and season with sea salt. Cook, stirring, for a few minutes more, until the squid is lightly browned.

Toss the rocket with the olive oil and lemon juice, then arrange in the centre of 4 serving plates. Pile the squid on top and serve immediately.

GARLIC CHILLI PRAWNS

SERVES FOUR

INGREDIENTS

1 kg (2 lb 3 oz) raw prawns
    (shrimps)
2 garlic bulbs
125 ml (4 fl oz) olive oil
4 long red chillies, sliced
sea salt
freshly cracked black pepper
2 handfuls flat-leaf parsley,
    chopped
lemon wedges to serve

METHOD

Peel and devein the prawns, leaving the tails on. Separate the garlic cloves, then peel and chop them.

Heat the olive oil in a frying pan. Cook the garlic and chilli over low heat until soft but not browned, about 5 minutes. Add the prawns, season with sea salt and black pepper and cook for 2 minutes on each side, or until they just turn white.

Stir the chopped parsley into the prawns. Serve immediately, with lemon wedges and a green salad.

ZUCCHINI FRITTERS

SERVES FOUR

INGREDIENTS

3 zucchini (courgettes), coarsely
   grated
sea salt
1 large onion, finely diced
4 handfuls flat-leaf parsley,
   chopped
1 handful dill, chopped
3 tablespoons plain (all-purpose)
   flour
2 eggs, lightly beaten
freshly cracked black pepper
250 ml (8½ fl oz) sunflower or
   canola oil
garlic yoghurt (see page 185)
   to serve

METHOD

Put the grated zucchini in a colander, sprinkle with sea salt and allow
the liquid to drain for 20 minutes. Squeeze the excess liquid from the
zucchini and transfer to a bowl.

Add the onion, parsley, dill, flour and eggs to the zucchini and mix to
combine. Season with sea salt and black pepper.

Heat the oil in a non-stick frying pan. Drop 1 tablespoon of the mixture
at a time into the oil and cook over high heat for 2–3 minutes, or until
golden brown on both sides. Drain on paper towel and serve hot or
cold, with garlic yoghurt and a green salad.

TURKISH BAKED BEANS

SERVES FOUR

INGREDIENTS

250 g (9 oz) dried red kidney
　beans
125 ml (4 fl oz) extra-virgin
　olive oil
1 onion, diced
3 garlic cloves
650 g (1 lb 7 oz) tomatoes,
　chopped
2 tablespoons Turkish pepper
　paste (see page 187)
1 handful thyme sprigs
pinch of sugar
sea salt
freshly cracked black pepper
1 small handful flat-leaf parsley
lemon wedges to serve
Turkish bread to serve

METHOD

Soak the kidney beans in cold water for at least 8 hours. Drain the beans, place in a saucepan and cover with plenty of water. Bring to the boil and cook for 1 hour, or until the beans are tender, then drain.

Heat the oil in a heavy-based saucepan and fry the onion over medium heat for 10–15 minutes, or until soft but not browned. Add the drained kidney beans, whole garlic cloves and tomato, then cover and bring to the boil. Reduce the heat and stir in the pepper paste, thyme and sugar. Season with sea salt and black pepper and cook, covered, for 1 hour, or until the beans are soft.

Sprinkle the beans with the parsley and serve with the lemon wedges and warm crusty Turkish bread.

NOTE

You can also used canned chopped tomatoes.

BAKED EGGPLANT WITH CHICKEN

SERVES FOUR

INGREDIENTS

2 eggplants (aubergines)
125 ml (4 fl oz) extra-virgin
    olive oil
1 large brown onion, diced
300 g (10½ oz) chicken thighs,
    chopped
1 green capsicum (pepper), diced
1 green chilli, chopped
4 tomatoes, diced
2 handfuls flat-leaf parsley,
    chopped
2 tablespoons Turkish pepper
    paste (see page 187)
sea salt
freshly cracked black pepper

METHOD

Preheat the oven to 160°C (320°F/Gas 2–3). Peel the eggplants in strips to give them a striped appearance. Cut them in half lengthwise and brush with some of the olive oil. Cook the eggplant in a frying pan over high heat for 5 minutes each side, or until golden. Transfer the eggplant to an ovenproof dish and bake for 10 minutes, or until soft.

Meanwhile, heat the remaining olive oil in a frying pan. Fry the onion over medium heat for 10–15 minutes, or until soft but not browned. Add the chicken, capsicum and chilli and cook for 15 minutes, or until the mixture is thick. Add the tomato, parsley and pepper paste, season to taste with sea salt and black pepper and cook for 15–20 minutes, or until tender.

Sprinkle the eggplant with a little salt. Spoon the chicken mixture over the eggplant and bake for another 10 minutes.

RED LENTIL SOUP

SERVES FOUR

INGREDIENTS

50 g (2 oz) butter

3 tablespoons extra-virgin olive oil

2 onions, finely diced

2 tablespoons Turkish pepper
   paste (see page 187)

3 tablespoons tomato paste

200 g (7 oz) red lentils, washed

500 g (1 lb 2 oz) chopped
   tomatoes

2 handfuls flat-leaf parsley,
   chopped

1.25 litres (42 fl oz) vegetable
   stock or water

sea salt

freshly cracked black pepper

METHOD

Heat the butter and olive oil in a large saucepan and sauté the onion for 5–10 minutes, or until golden. Add the pepper paste and tomato paste and cook for 2–3 minutes, then add the red lentils, tomato and parsley, and cook, stirring constantly, for 3 minutes.

Add the stock or water and gently simmer for 20 minutes, or until thickened. Season to taste with sea salt and cracked black pepper.

VARIATIONS

This is a traditional recipe, but you can also add pumpkin, carrot, celery, chillies or whatever vegetables you have on hand. The soup will thicken as it cools. It can be thinned down with water or stock.

I like to fry a handful of oregano leaves, a handful of mint leaves, 2 tablespoons of paprika and a pinch of salt in 125 ml (4 fl oz) olive oil until the leaves are crispy, and drizzle it over the soup to serve.

CHICKEN AND COUSCOUS SALAD

SERVES FOUR

INGREDIENTS

250 ml (8$^1/_2$ fl oz) chicken stock

2 cups couscous

pinch of sea salt

pinch of freshly cracked black
   pepper

olive oil, for cooking

300 g (10$^1/_2$ oz) chicken thighs,
   chopped

200 g (7 oz) sweet potato, cut into
   1 cm ($^1/_2$ in) cubes

3 tablespoons extra-virgin olive oil

2 tablespoons pomegranate
   molasses (see page 186)

2 handfuls mint leaves

2 handfuls coriander (cilantro)
   leaves

1 tomato, diced

10 spring onions (scallions),
   chopped

2 green chillies, finely chopped

pinch of ground cinnamon

METHOD

Heat the stock in a saucepan until boiling. Stir in the couscous, sea salt and black pepper. Turn off the heat, cover and set aside for 10 minutes, or until tender. Fluff up the couscous with a fork.

Heat a little olive oil in a frying pan. Cook the chicken over high heat for 3–4 minutes each side, or until cooked through.

In a separate frying pan, heat a little more olive oil. Cook the sweet potato, stirring, for about 10 minutes, or until golden brown and soft in the centre.

Combine the extra-virgin olive oil and pomegranate molasses in a large bowl. Shred the chicken and add to the bowl. Fold in the sweet potato, mint, coriander, tomato, spring onion, chilli and cinnamon.

Gently fold the couscous through the salad, and serve immediately.

LEEK AND PARMESAN TART

SERVES EIGHT

INGREDIENTS

Shortcrust pastry
180 g (6 oz) unsalted butter
240 g (8½ oz) plain (all-purpose) flour
pinch of sea salt

Filling
20 g (¾ oz) butter
3 leeks, finely chopped
5 eggs
250 ml (8½ fl oz) thickened (double/thick) cream (45% fat)
3 handfuls flat-leaf parsley, chopped
sea salt
freshly cracked black pepper
150 g (5 oz) parmesan, grated

METHOD

To make the pastry, mix the butter, flour and sea salt in a food processor until it resembles breadcrumbs. Add 3 tablespoons of cold water and blend until the dough comes together into a ball. Roll out the dough on a lightly floured surface to line a 30 cm (12 in) flan tin. Refrigerate the pastry for 30 minutes. Preheat the oven to 160°C (320°F/Gas 2–3).

Line the pastry with a sheet of baking paper and fill with a layer of baking beads or rice. Bake for 15 minutes, then remove the paper and beads and bake for another 10 minutes, or until the pastry is golden.

To make the filling, melt the butter in a frying pan over high heat and cook the leek until it caramelises, about 10 minutes. Combine the eggs, cream and parsley in a bowl and season with sea salt and black pepper.

Spread the leek over the pastry base, sprinkle with the parmesan and then pour the egg mixture over the top. Bake for about 30 minutes, or until just firm. Serve hot with a garden salad.

DESSERTS

AFTER DINNER IS THE TIME FOR TURKISH FAMILIES TO RELAX AND SPEND HOURS ENGAGING IN LIVELY CONVERSATION, SIPPING TEA AND NIBBLING ON SWEET CAKES, STICKY BAKLAVA, NUTS AND DRIED FRUIT.

CARAMELISED FIGS

SERVES FOUR

INGREDIENTS

150 g (5 oz) hazelnuts
½ cup caster (superfine) sugar
4 figs, halved lengthwise
hazelnut ice-cream to serve

METHOD

Preheat the oven to 160°C (320°F/Gas 2–3). Roast the hazelnuts on a baking tray for 10 minutes, or until fragrant. Rub the hazelnuts in a clean tea towel to remove the skins, then roughly chop them.

Place a frying pan over high heat. Sprinkle the sugar over the base of the hot pan and place the figs, cut-side down, on top of the sugar. Cook the figs for 1–2 minutes, or until they start to caramelise (they will start to smoke a little). Turn the figs and cook for 1–2 seconds.

Place the figs on serving plates and serve immediately, with the hazelnut ice-cream and chopped hazelnuts.

NOTE

The figs should be perfectly ripe for this recipe.

POPPYSEED CAKE

INGREDIENTS

200 g (7 oz) poppyseeds
1 cup self-raising flour
1 teaspoon baking powder
pinch of salt
2 eggs
1 cup caster (superfine) sugar
1 tablespoon lemon zest
125 ml (4 fl oz) milk
125 g (4 oz) unsalted butter,
  melted
2 tablespoons olive oil
cream or yoghurt to serve

METHOD

Preheat the oven to 160°C (320°F/Gas 2–3). Grease and flour a 27 cm (11 in) springform tin.

Stir the poppyseeds in a dry frying pan over high heat for 5–10 minutes, or until fragrant. Use a mortar and pestle to grind the seeds until fine.

Sift together the flour, baking powder and salt. Beat the eggs and sugar until pale. Stir in the crushed poppyseeds and lemon zest. Fold the sifted dry ingredients into the egg mixture in three batches, alternating with the milk. Fold in the melted butter and olive oil.

Pour the mixture into the cake tin. Bake for 40 minutes, or until a skewer inserted into the cake comes out clean. Leave the cake in the tin to cool. Serve at room temperature, with cream or yoghurt.

BAKED QUINCES WITH YOGHURT AND PISTACHIOS

INGREDIENTS

100 g (3½ oz) pistachios

2 kg (4 lb 7 oz) quinces

2 cups sugar

250 g (9 oz) Greek-style plain
  yoghurt

METHOD

Preheat the oven to 160°C (320°F/Gas 2–3). Spread the pistachios on a baking tray. Roast for 10 minutes, or until fragrant. Roughly chop the cooled pistachios.

Increase the oven to 180°C (350°F/Gas 4). Wash and scrub the quinces, then cut them in half and place them in a baking dish, cut-side down. Sprinkle the quinces with the sugar and 750 ml (25 fl oz) water. Cover with a sheet of foil and bake for 2 hours. Turn the quinces over and bake for a further 1 hour, checking that they don't burn. The quinces should be ruby coloured when they are cooked.

Remove the cores from the quinces. Spoon the quinces into serving bowls and top with the yoghurt and pistachios.

NOTE

Store any leftover quinces in an airtight jar in the refrigerator for up to a week. Serve for breakfast or dessert.

TURKISH YOGHURT AND OLIVE OIL CAKE

SERVES TEN

INGREDIENTS

3 eggs

1¹/₂ cups caster (superfine) sugar

250 g (9 oz) Greek-style plain
   yoghurt

250 ml (8¹/₂ fl oz) olive oil

2 cups self-raising flour

icing (confectioner's) sugar,
   for dusting

METHOD

Preheat the oven to 160°C (320°F/Gas 2–3). Grease and flour a 27 cm (11 in) springform tin.

Beat the eggs and sugar until pale. Stir in the yoghurt and olive oil. Add the flour and mix well.

Pour the mixture into the cake tin. Bake for about 1 hour, or until a skewer inserted into the cake comes out clean. Serve the cake hot or at room temperature, dusted with icing sugar.

PEAR AND HAZELNUT CAKE

SERVES TEN

INGREDIENTS

150 g (5 oz) hazelnuts

3 pears

3 eggs

1½ cups caster (superfine) sugar

125 ml (4 fl oz) olive oil

150 g (5 oz) unsalted butter, melted

½ cup semolina

1 teaspoon ground cinnamon

250 g (9 oz) Greek-style plain yoghurt

2 cups self-raising flour

METHOD

Preheat the oven to 160°C (320°F/Gas 2–3). Grease and flour a 27 cm (11 in) springform tin.

Roast the hazelnuts on a baking tray for 10 minutes, or until fragrant. Rub the hazelnuts in a clean tea towel to remove the skins, then crush them in a food processor.

Peel the pears and cut them into chunks.

Beat the eggs and sugar until pale. Stir in the olive oil, butter, semolina and cinnamon, then stir in the yoghurt. Fold in the flour, and then fold in the pear.

Pour the mixture into the cake tin and sprinkle the hazelnuts over the top. Bake for 40 minutes, or until a skewer inserted into the cake comes out clean. Leave in the tin to cool. Serve the cake at room temperature.

LIME AND POLENTA CAKE

SERVES TEN

INGREDIENTS

Lime syrup
250 ml (8½ fl oz) lime juice
1 cup sugar

120 g (4 oz) unsalted butter
200 g (7 oz) sugar
zest and juice of 2 limes
3 eggs
1 cup polenta
250 g (9 oz) Greek-style plain
  yoghurt
2 cups self-raising flour
cream or yoghurt to serve

METHOD

Preheat the oven to 160°C (320°F/Gas 2–3). Grease and flour a 27 cm (11 in) springform tin.

To make the lime syrup, combine the lime juice and sugar in a saucepan. Bring to the boil and cook until the sugar dissolves, about 5 minutes. Set aside to cool.

Beat the butter, sugar and lime zest in a food processor until pale. Add the eggs, one a time, with the motor running. Beat well. Blend in the lime juice, polenta and yoghurt, then fold in the flour.

Pour the mixture into the cake tin. Bake for 40 minutes, or until a skewer inserted into the cake comes out clean.

Pour the cold syrup over the hot cake. Leave in the tin to cool. Serve the cake at room temperature, with cream or yoghurt.

SEMOLINA HALVA

SERVES FOUR

INGREDIENTS

100 g (3½ oz) pine nuts
20 g (¾ oz) unsalted butter
1 cup semolina
500 ml (17 fl oz) milk
1 cup sugar

METHOD

Stir the pine nuts in a dry frying pan over high heat until golden.

Put the butter and semolina in a non-stick frying pan and cook, stirring constantly, for 15 minutes. Add the toasted pine nuts and cook, stirring, for 5–10 minutes, or until browned.

Put the milk and sugar in a saucepan and stir until the sugar has dissolved. Bring to the boil, then carefully pour the milk mixture over the semolina mixture and stir until thoroughly combined. Take care when adding the milk because the semolina mixture will bubble up.

Allow the halva to stand for 20 minutes, then spoon it into bowls and serve at room temperature.

NOTE

This is a beautiful comfort food, and is perfect for breakfast as well as dessert.

Halva is made to commemorate the passing of loved ones, and in memory of the joy they brought to the family and community. I make this on the anniversary of the loss of my brother, Murat, and share it with my customers, friends and suppliers. It makes me think of his beautiful smile, which I will hold close to my heart forever.

YOGHURT AND RASPBERRY CAKE

SERVES TEN

INGREDIENTS

150 g (5 oz) unsalted butter, softened

1½ cups sugar

3 eggs

250 g (9 oz) Greek-style plain yoghurt

zest and juice of 1 lemon

2 cups self-raising flour

1 teaspoon bicarbonate of soda (baking soda)

250 g (9 oz) frozen raspberries

METHOD

Preheat the oven to 160°C (320°F/Gas 2–3). Grease and flour a 27 cm (11 in) springform tin.

Beat the butter and sugar in a food processor until pale. Add the eggs, one at a time, and beat well. Fold in the yoghurt, lemon zest and lemon juice, then fold in the flour and bicarbonate of soda.

Pour half the batter into the cake tin. Sprinkle the frozen raspberries over the batter, then pour in the remaining batter. Bake for 40 minutes, or until a skewer inserted into the cake comes out clean. Leave in the tin to cool. Serve the cake at room temperature.

VARIATION

You can replace the raspberries with any frozen berries.

ORANGE AND SEMOLINA CAKE

INGREDIENTS

3 eggs

1 cup sugar

140 g (5 oz) unsalted butter, melted

3 tablespoons olive oil

250 g (9 oz) Greek-style plain yoghurt

grated zest of 3 oranges

1/2 cup semolina

1 teaspoon baking powder

2 cups self-raising flour

3 tablespoons crushed pistachios

METHOD

Preheat the oven to 160°C (320°F/Gas 2–3). Grease and flour a 27 cm (11 in) springform tin.

Beat the eggs and sugar together until pale, then beat in the butter and olive oil. Add the yoghurt, orange zest, semolina and baking powder and mix well. Fold in the flour.

Pour the mixture into the cake tin and sprinkle the pistachios on top. Bake for 40 minutes, or until a skewer inserted into the cake comes out clean. Leave in the tin to cool. Serve the cake at room temperature.

PEAR AND RAISIN CRUMBLE

SERVES SIX

INGREDIENTS

250 g (9 oz) hazelnuts

1$\frac{1}{2}$ cups loosely packed brown
sugar

1 kg (2 lb 3 oz) ripe pears, peeled
and roughly chopped

150 g (5 oz) raisins

2 tablespoons ground cinnamon

300 g (10$\frac{1}{2}$ oz) rolled oats

250 g (9 oz) unsalted butter,
melted

yoghurt, cream or ice cream
to serve

METHOD

Preheat the oven to 160°C (320°F/Gas 2–3). Roast the hazelnuts on a baking tray for 10 minutes, or until fragrant. Rub the hazelnuts in a clean tea towel to remove the skins, then roughly chop them.

Put $\frac{1}{2}$ cup of the brown sugar in a bowl. Add the pears, raisins and cinnamon and toss until thoroughly combined. Transfer the mixture to a 35 x 10 cm (14 x 4 in) loaf tin.

In the same bowl, mix the rolled oats, hazelnuts, remaining brown sugar and the melted butter. Spoon the oat mixture over the pear and raisin mixture and then pat it down. Bake for 30 minutes, or until the topping is crunchy and the pears are soft. Serve warm, with yoghurt, cream or ice cream.

PRUNE AND ALMOND CAKE

SERVES TEN

INGREDIENTS

200 g (7 oz) ground almonds
120 g (4 oz) unsalted butter,
 softened
1 cup sugar
2 eggs
1/2 teaspoon almond essence
250 g (9 oz) pitted prunes

METHOD

Preheat the oven to 160°C (320°F/Gas 2–3). Grease and flour a 27 cm (11 in) springform tin.

Stir the almonds in a dry frying pan over high heat for 5–10 minutes, or until fragrant. Set aside to cool.

Cream the butter and sugar in a food processor until pale. Add the eggs, ground almonds and almond essence and mix well.

Pour the mixture into the cake tin and arrange the prunes on top. Bake for 40 minutes, or until a skewer inserted into the cake comes out clean. Leave in the tin to cool. Serve at room temperature.

BLUEBERRY AND POLENTA CAKE

SERVES TEN

INGREDIENTS

3 eggs

1½ cups sugar

250 ml (8½ fl oz) olive oil

50 g (2 oz) unsalted butter, melted

250 g (9 oz) Greek-style plain
  yoghurt

1 cup polenta

zest and juice of 1 lime

1½ cups self-raising flour

1 teaspoon baking powder

250 g (9 oz) blueberries

METHOD

Preheat the oven to 160°C (320°F/Gas 2–3). Grease and flour a 27 cm (11 in) springform tin.

Beat the eggs and sugar until pale, then beat in the olive oil and melted butter. Add the yoghurt, polenta, lime zest and juice and mix well. Fold in the flour and baking powder.

Pour half the batter into the cake tin. Sprinkle the blueberries over the batter, then pour in the remaining batter. Bake for 40 minutes, or until a skewer inserted into the cake comes out clean. Leave in the tin to cool. Serve the cake at room temperature.

CHOCOLATE MOUSSE CAKE

INGREDIENTS

250 g (9 oz) dark chocolate
(70% cocoa)
250 g (9 oz) unsalted butter
100 g ($3^{1}/_{2}$ oz) ground hazelnuts
8 eggs, separated
250 g (9 oz) caster (superfine)
sugar
pomegranate seeds to serve

METHOD

Preheat the oven to 180°C (350°F/Gas 4). Grease a 27 cm (11 in) springform tin.

Bring a small saucepan of water to the boil, then remove from the heat. Place the chocolate and butter in a heatproof bowl. Sit the bowl over the pan of water and stir until the mixture is melted and smooth. Set aside to cool.

Stir the ground hazelnuts in a dry frying pan over high heat for 5–10 minutes, or until fragrant. Set aside to cool.

Put the egg whites in one large bowl and put the egg yolks in another large bowl. Add half the sugar to the egg whites and add the remainder to the egg yolks. Whisk the egg whites and sugar until soft peaks form. Whisk the egg yolks and sugar until the mixture is pale and creamy and the sugar has dissolved.

Fold the chocolate mixture and hazelnuts into the egg yolk mixture. Gently fold the egg whites through the chocolate mixture.

Spoon the mixture into the cake tin and bake for 10 minutes, or until just set. It will still be a little wobbly, but will set when chilled. Turn off the oven and cool the cake with the door open to prevent sinking. Refrigerate the cake in the tin. Serve chilled, sprinkled with the pomegranate seeds, if desired.

POACHED FIGS WITH WALNUTS AND CREAM

SERVES FOUR

INGREDIENTS

500 g (1 lb 2 oz) Turkish dried figs
50 g (2 oz) walnuts
2 tablespoons sugar
juice of $1/2$ lemon
cream or yoghurt to serve

METHOD

Soak the dried figs in hot water for 1 hour.

Meanwhile, preheat the oven to 160°C (320°F/Gas 2–3). Roast the walnuts on a baking tray for 10 minutes, or until fragrant.

Drain the figs and transfer to a saucepan. Add the sugar, lemon juice and enough water to just cover the figs. Bring to a gentle simmer and cook for 10 minutes, or until the figs are just soft. Remove the figs with a slotted spoon.

Gently cook the poaching liquid for about 10 minutes, until reduced and syrupy, then set aside until cool.

Once the figs are cool enough to handle, split them open at the base. Push a walnut inside each fig. Stand the figs on serving plates and drizzle with the syrup. Serve with cream or yoghurt.

PASSIONFRUIT AND POLENTA CAKE

INGREDIENTS

250 g (9 oz) passionfruit pulp

2 cups sugar

3 eggs

125 g (4 oz) Greek-style plain
  yoghurt

100 g ($3^1/2$ oz) unsalted butter,
  melted

3 tablespoons olive oil

1 cup polenta

$1^1/2$ cups self-raising flour

1 tablespoon baking powder

METHOD

Preheat the oven to 160°C (320°F/Gas 2–3). Grease and flour a 27 cm (11 in) springform tin.

Combine the passionfruit pulp, 1 cup of the sugar and 3 tablespoons water in a saucepan. Cook the syrup for about 5 minutes, or until it comes to the boil. Set aside to cool.

Beat the eggs and remaining sugar together until pale and creamy. Add the yoghurt, butter, oil and polenta and mix until thoroughly combined. Fold in the flour and baking powder.

Pour the mixture into the tin. Bake for 40 minutes, or until a skewer inserted into the cake comes out clean. Pour the cold syrup over the hot cake. Leave in the tin to cool. Serve at room temperature.

VANILLA BEAN CHEESECAKE

SERVES TEN TO TWELVE

INGREDIENTS

½ cup roasted hazelnuts

200 g (7 oz) shortbread biscuits (cookies)

80 g (3 oz) unsalted butter, melted

6 eggs

400 g (14 oz) cream cheese, softened

125 g (4 oz) Greek-style plain yoghurt

125 ml (4 fl oz) single (light) cream (35% fat)

250 g (9 oz) sugar

1 vanilla bean, scraped

METHOD

Preheat the oven to 160°C (320°F/Gas 2–3). Roast the hazelnuts on a baking tray for 10 minutes, or until fragrant. Rub the hazelnuts in a clean tea towel to remove the skins, then chop them. Reduce the oven to 140°C (275°F/Gas 1).

Combine the biscuits and butter in a food processor until fine crumbs form. Stir in the chopped hazelnuts. Press the biscuit mixture over the base of a 27 cm (11 in) springform tin. Refrigerate for 15 minutes while you prepare the filling.

Blend the eggs, cream cheese, yoghurt, cream, sugar and vanilla bean seeds in a food processor until smooth. Pour over the biscuit base and bake for 45 minutes, or until just firm but still slightly wobbly. Cool in the tin, then refrigerate for about 3 hours before serving.

VARIATION

You can use gluten-free biscuits (cookies) to make the base.

FIG AND HAZELNUT CAKE

SERVES TEN

INGREDIENTS

150 g (5 oz) hazelnuts
3 eggs
1½ cups sugar
250 ml (8½ fl oz) olive oil
250 g (9 oz) Greek-style plain
  yoghurt
5 figs, chopped (see Note)
2 cups self-raising flour
1 teaspoon baking powder

METHOD

Preheat the oven to 160°C (320°F/Gas 2–3). Grease and flour a 27 cm (11 in) springform tin.

Roast the hazelnuts on a baking tray for 10 minutes, or until fragrant. Rub the hazelnuts in a clean tea towel to remove the skins, then finely chop them.

Beat the eggs and sugar together until pale. Stir in the olive oil, yoghurt, figs and hazelnuts. Add the flour and baking powder and mix well.

Pour the mixture into the cake tin. Bake for about 30 minutes, or until a skewer inserted into the cake comes out clean. Leave in the tin to cool. Serve the cake at room temperature.

NOTE

If fresh figs aren't available, use 6 dried figs. Soak them in hot water for 10 minutes before draining and chopping them.

BAKLAVA

MAKES ABOUT FIFTY PIECES

INGREDIENTS
200 g (7 oz) pistachios
250 g (9 oz) unsalted butter,
  melted
20 sheets (about 375 g/13 oz)
  filo pastry
250 g (9 oz) chopped walnuts

Syrup
1$\frac{1}{2}$ cups sugar
juice of $\frac{1}{4}$ lemon

METHOD
Preheat the oven to 160°C (320°F/Gas 2–3). Spread the pistachios on a baking tray. Roast for 10 minutes, or until fragrant. Finely chop the cooled pistachios.

To make the syrup, mix the sugar, lemon juice and 250 ml (8$\frac{1}{2}$ fl oz) water in a saucepan. Bring to the boil, then cook for 10–15 minutes, or until the syrup is thickened and holds its shape when dropped from a spoon. Set aside to cool.

Brush a 25 x 40 x 2 cm (10 x 16 x $\frac{3}{4}$ in) baking tray with some melted butter. Lay a sheet of filo pastry on the tray and lightly brush all over with melted butter. Repeat until you have used 10 sheets of pastry. Sprinkle the walnuts over the pastry. Lay a sheet of pastry on top of the walnuts and lightly brush all over with melted butter. Repeat until you have used the remaining pastry, then refrigerate for 10 minutes.

Using a very sharp knife, cut through the pastry to make strips 4 cm (1$\frac{1}{2}$ in) wide, then cut across the pastry on an angle to make diamond shapes. Bake for 30 minutes, or until the pastry is golden. Drizzle the cold syrup over the hot baklava and sprinkle with the pistachios.

BASICS

PEELING TOMATOES

Score a cross in the base of a ripe tomato. Put the tomato in a heatproof bowl and cover with boiling water for about 10 seconds. Plunge into cold water, then peel the skin away from the cross.

STERILISING JARS

Wash the glass jars, rinse them in very hot water and drain thoroughly. Boil the lids or rinse them in very hot water. Do not wipe the jars or lids with a tea towel. Place the jars, upside down, on a rack in a warm oven for about 30 minutes. Use tongs to handle the hot jars and lids.

AYRAN

INGREDIENTS

500 g (1 lb 2 oz) Greek-style plain yoghurt
pinch of salt

METHOD

Whisk the yoghurt and salt with 250 ml ($8^{1}/_{2}$ fl oz) water. Serve chilled.

NOTE

This is a traditional Turkish drink that is served with lunch or dinner, or when guests come to visit.

GARLIC YOGHURT

INGREDIENTS

1 garlic clove
pinch of sea salt
250 g (9 oz) Greek-style plain yoghurt

METHOD

Use a mortar and pestle to crush the garlic with the sea salt until it forms a paste. Gently fold the paste through the yoghurt.

GLOSSARY

BAHARAT

Meaning 'to throw spring into a dish' in Turkish, baharat is a spice mix used in North Africa and the Middle East. Turkish baharat contains mint as well as the traditional pepper, cumin, coriander, cloves, nutmeg, cardamom and cinnamon.

NIGELLA SEEDS

Also known as kalonji (or *çörekotu* in Turkey), nigella seeds are tiny black seeds with a nutty, peppery flavour. They are used as a seasoning in India and the Middle East, particularly with vegetables and breads.

POMEGRANATE MOLASSES

This concentrated, thick syrup made from the juice of pomegranates is used in sauces, dressings and marinades. It has a dark red colour and a tart, slightly sweet flavour. Found in Mediterranean and Middle Eastern cuisines.

PURSLANE

Purslane or 'pigweed' is known as *semizotu* in Turkey. Considered a weed in many countries, purslane has an excellent nutritional content, with high levels of omega-3 fatty acids, vitamins and minerals. It can be eaten fresh or cooked.

SUCUK

Sucuk is a spicy Turkish beef sausage that contains paprika, chilli, garlic and pepper.

SUMAC

A ground dark-red spice from the berries of a shrub that grows wild throughout Italy and the Middle East, sumac is widely used in cooking to add tartness to dishes such as kebabs, fish, vegetables or eggs.

TURKISH PEPPER PASTE

Made from long red chillies that have been minced (ground) and then sun-dried, this thick red paste is used as a flavour enhancer or savoury spread. It is available in a hot variety and a sweet variety, and can be replaced with tomato paste.

INDEX

ACKNOWLEDGEMENTS

I am grateful to Anne and the women of Turkey who created amazing recipes from very limited ingredients, and to Baba and the men of Turkey who worked hard to provide for their families.

I am also grateful to my beautiful sister, Güfer, who has always worked hard and always been my friend.

Robert and Sally Molines, thank you for inspiring me and for being my great friends.

Fiona Hardie and Sandy Grant, thank you for making a dream come true for a little Turk. I feel like a big Turk now.

Thank you Michelle Fenton and Meaghan Vosz for endless typing and always being there for me. I love you like sisters.

Christine Gibson, artist and great friend, thank you for your friendship and for painting my restaurants.

Rowena Cornwell, you are a great friend. Thank you for renovating my house and making my life pretty.

Elea Bernou, thank you for teaching me English all those years ago.

Thank you, Lisa Dempsey of Jac + Jack, for being my soul sister and supplying the beautiful clothes for me to wear for photography.

Ernesto Ellem, thank you for your wonderful support over many years.

Paul McNally and Heather Menzies, thank you for loving my house and using it as a stage for photography, and thank you for loving my broad (fava) beans. Alicia Taylor, Sarah DeNardi, Vivien Valk and Justine Harding, thank you all for your work on my book.

Thank you to every customer who has come through the doors of my café. Thank you for your support over many years, and for sharing my happiness and sadness. I still have a small family in Turkey, but I have a big family in Australia.

Every recipe is sprinkled with something of me. It is up to you, my readers, to sprinkle them with something of you as you prepare them for those you love.

An SBS Book

Published in 2012 by Hardie Grant Books

Hardie Grant Books (Australia)
Ground Floor, Building 1
658 Church Street
Richmond, Victoria 3121
www.hardiegrant.com.au

Hardie Grant Books (UK)
Second Floor, North Suite
Dudley House
Southampton Street
London WC2E 7HF
www.hardiegrant.co.uk

Cataloguing-in-Publication data is available from the National Library of Australia.

ISBN 9781742702674

Publishing director: Paul McNally
Project manager and editor: Justine Harding
Design manager: Heather Menzies
Designer: Vivien Valk
Photographer: Alicia Taylor
Food stylist: Sarah DeNardi

Colour reproduction by Splitting Image Colour Studio
Printed in China by 1010 Printing International Limited

Recipes were tested using a fan-forced oven. All recipes use free-range eggs.